CLEARLY DELICIOUS

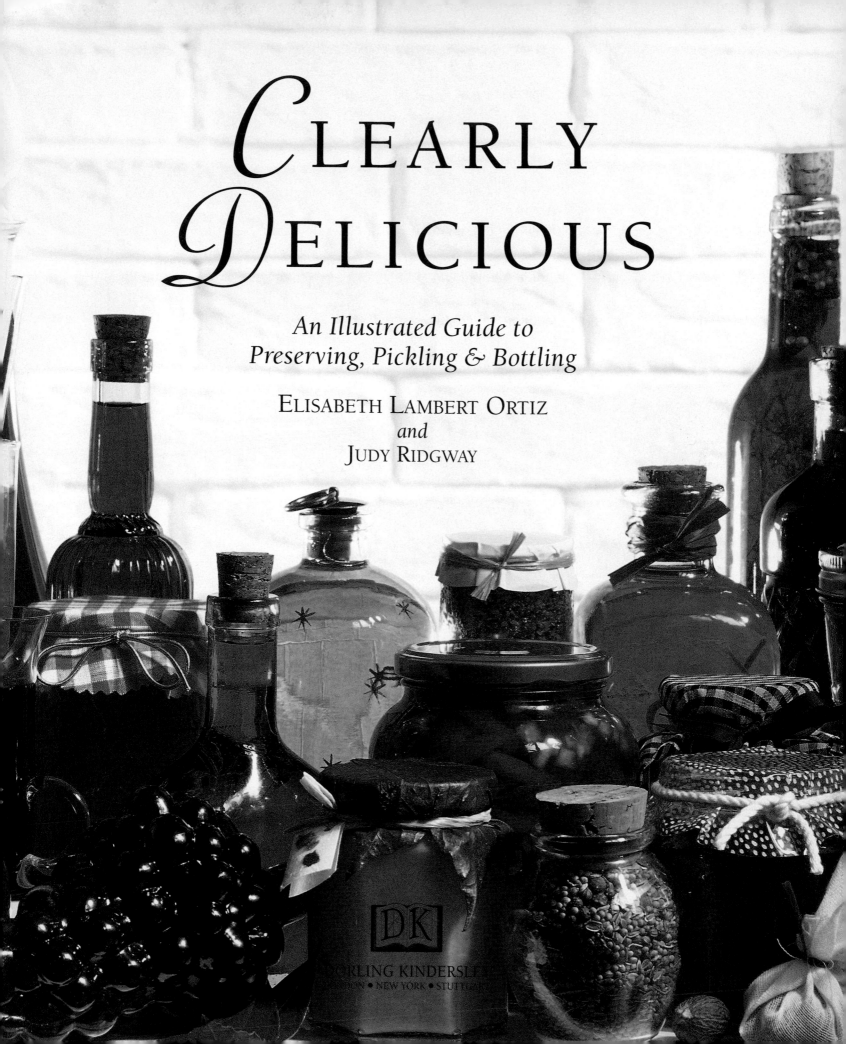

CLEARLY
DELICIOUS

An Illustrated Guide to
Preserving, Pickling & Bottling

ELISABETH LAMBERT ORTIZ
and
JUDY RIDGWAY

DK

DORLING KINDERSLEY
LONDON • NEW YORK • STUTTGART

A DORLING KINDERSLEY BOOK

Created and produced by
CARROLL & BROWN LIMITED
5 Lonsdale Road
London NW6 6RA

Editorial Director Jeni Wright
Editors Julia Alcock
Angela Nilsen

Art Editor Chrissie Lloyd
Designers Carmel O'Neill
Michael Dyer
Production Wendy Rogers
Amanda Mackie

First published in Great Britain in 1994
by Dorling Kindersley Limited,
9 Henrietta Street, London WC2E 8PS
Copyright © 1994 Carroll & Brown, London

A CIP catalogue record for this book is available from the
British Library.

ISBN 0 7513 0090 X

Reproduced by Colourscan, Singapore
Printed in Singapore by Toppan Printing

FOREWORD

THE ART OF PRESERVING can turn an ordinary storecupboard or pantry into an Aladdin's cave of good things – beautiful to look at, luscious to eat, and a joy both to give and receive. It can also turn your refrigerator and freezer into a rescue service for emergiences like anniversaries – when presents are obligatory, but unbought. The kitchen is a cheerful place, and though undeniably there is work involved in transforming fruits into jams and jellies, and vegetables into pickles and chutneys, there is no need for lonely drudgery when it comes to preserving. Family, and often friends, like to join in, and what started as a kitchen chore can turn into a celebration with everyone, not just the cook, having fun.

Being creative and economical at the same time can bring a glow of virtue to even the most modest cheek. But sometimes imagination flags and the cook is bereft of ideas for a meal that is looming. An array of preserves in the storecupboard, refrigerator or freezer will stimulate culinary wits, and new dishes may well be created by the challenge these good things pose: new flavours to liven up dull ordinary dishes or simply help familiar ones that need a lift.

The conservation-minded can take special pleasure from re-using jars, bottles, tins, and boxes that would otherwise clutter up kitchen shelves, uselessly reproachful. Those artistically gifted with clever fingers can do wonders with gift wrapping, decorating glass jars and bottles, and transforming tins and baskets with ingenuity but little cost. Wrapping paper, labels and tags, ribbons, and cord can all be recruited to help the container be worthy of its contents.

As the Spanish saying has it: *"es mas bueno el vino en bella copa"* – the wine is better in a beautiful glass.

ELISABETH LAMBERT ORTIZ

Jams, Jellies & Other Sweet Concoctions

JAMS

SUMMER HERALDS the joyous beginning of jam making, when the house is filled with the perfume of simmering fruits being transformed by sugar and heat into a luscious spread. Jam turns bread into a luxury, and is a useful ingredient in sauces, puddings, and desserts, as well as in cake and cookie making. There is hardly a sight more enticing than an abundance of fruits waiting to be transformed into jam. With a great cornucopia of fruits to choose from, swelling and ripening in a tantalizing succession of harvests, throughout summer and autumn, there is plenty of room for experimentation.

Although familiar fruits, such as raspberries and blackcurrants, still provide the most popular jams, less traditional flavours can be created with pineapples, or apples and ginger. Indeed, part of the fun when filling jars with the finished jam, is to admire the colours produced by the clever blending of fruits. Rhubarb and strawberries, for instance, combine to make a beautiful rose-red confection, pleasing both eye and palate.

MAKING JAMS

❦ Choose the ingredients. Jam is made with two main ingredients – fruit and sugar. The fruits must contain the right proportions of pectin and acid so that the jam can set properly, and enough sugar must be added to preserve it. (Pectin is a natural strengthening substance found only in fruits). Fruits that are fresh and slightly under-ripe contain the most pectin, so buy or pick the desired fruits when they are just coming into season. Over-ripe fruits contain very little pectin so they do not set well, and are better kept for making chutneys. Fruits high in both pectin and acid are apples, cranberries, gooseberries, currants, and damsons. Fruits that will set a jam moderately well are blackberries, greengages, apricots, loganberries, and raspberries. Cherries, pears, pineapples, nectarines, and some varieties of strawberry are poor setters and need the addition of pectin and acid to make a satisfactory jam. Fruits that do not have good setting properties can be used in combination with those that do, such as pears with damsons, and raspberries with redcurrants; these combinations may also require the addition of an acid, such as lemon juice. Alternatively, commercially bottled pectin can be useful for adding to jams made with ingredients low in pectin. It is important to add the correct amount, so follow the manufacturer's instructions carefully. Dried fruits like apricots make quite good jam, provided they have not been preserved with sulphur dioxide, which can affect the set. They need to be soaked for at least 24 hours before cooking. Some vegetables, such as marrows and carrots, can be used to make jam, but they need plenty of added lemon juice to ensure a reasonable set, and may require extra flavourings, such as spices.

❦ When it comes to the choice of sugar, both refined cane and beet granulated sugars work well, and there is no difference in the keeping qualities of jam made from either of these. However, lump and preserving sugar are better because they form less scum and they also give a slightly brighter, clearer jam. Commercially packaged sugar with pectin, sometimes called "jam sugar", is sugar that has been packed with natural apple pectin, especially for jam making. Follow the instructions on the package for best results.

❦ Other ingredients, such as nuts and a few tablespoons of liqueur or spirit, can be added to make the jam more interesting. These should be stirred in at the last minute after skimming the jam.

❦ Prepare the fruits. Remove any stems, leaves, mouldy or damaged parts. Wash lightly and pat dry with kitchen paper, to remove excess water. Stone fruits should be halved and stoned. Some recipes call for the addition of a few kernels and these can be extracted by cracking the stones with a hammer. Adding a few kernels will give the jam extra flavour, but too many will make the jam bitter. Blanch the kernels in boiling water and remove their skins before adding to the fruit.

❧ Weigh out the ingredients carefully, following either the metric or imperial measures. Do not mix the measurements because they are not interchangeable.

❧ Put the prepared fruits into a preserving pan with the recommended amount of water, and simmer until the fruits are soft. Generally, the mixture should reduce by about one-third before the sugar is added to ensure a good set. Start the juices running in soft fruits by crushing some of the fruits in the bottom of the pan.

❧ Warm the sugar (see box, page 20) while the fruits are cooking. Although this is not essential, the sugar will dissolve more quickly when warm rather than when cold. Make sure the fruit is really soft; if the sugar is added too soon, it will have a hardening effect on the fruits and this cannot be rectified. Add the sugar all at once and stir over a low heat until it has completely dissolved. A knob of butter can be added at this point to help reduce foaming, but this is not necessary. Increase the heat and bring to a boil, then to a simmer, stirring occasionally, until setting point is reached. Stir the jam as little as possible after the sugar has dissolved.

❧ Test the jam for set, removing it from the heat first to prevent over-cooking. The best way to test is with a sugar thermometer. If you can, clip the thermometer to the side of the pan when you start to cook the fruits. You will then be able to read the temperature as the jam progresses. If this is not possible, heat the thermometer in a jug of hot water. Stir the jam and immerse the bulb of the thermometer completely in the jam, taking care not to let it touch the bottom of the pan. When the thermometer reads 104°C (220°F), the jam should set if you have followed the recipe carefully.

❧ You can also test the jam by dropping a little on to a cold plate. Chill quickly in the refrigerator. If the jam forms a skin, and wrinkles when it is pushed with a finger or spoon, it should have reached setting point.

❧ When setting point is reached, lightly skim off any scum with a long-handled metal spoon. Pour the jam into warmed, dry sterilized jars (see page 11). Fill the jars to within 3 mm ($\frac{1}{8}$ inch) of the tops. If directed in the recipe, leave whole fruit jams to cool slightly before putting into jars, so that a thin skin forms and the fruits are evenly distributed through the jam.

How to seal and store

Seal the jars tightly, either with screw-top lids with plastic linings, or with ordinary metal or hard plastic twist-off lids. Jams can also be sealed with wax discs and cellophane circles. For this method, place the correct size of wax disc, wax-side down, on the surface of the jam. It should cover the jam exactly, and not run up the sides of the jar. Smooth over with a fingertip to remove any air pockets. Cover with a dampened cellophane circle and secure with a rubber band. Label the jars and keep in a cool dark place or in the refrigerator. Paper covers do not give such an airtight seal, so they are best for short-term storage only.

What can go wrong and why

A jam will crystallize if an over-concentration of sugar has been caused by excessive boiling. Jam can ferment or go mouldy if it contains too little sugar, or if it was not boiled sufficiently. This also happens in poor storage conditions, or through using over-ripe, wet, or bad fruits, or wet jars. If the jam is very dark, it has probably been boiled too fast at the first stage or too slow at the sugar stage. Storage in too bright a light also darkens jams. If setting point has not been reached, the jam will be runny. This can be corrected by re-boiling the runny jam. Alternatively, add a little sugar with pectin or liquid pectin (too much pectin will spoil the flavour of the jam). Other setting problems can be caused by a lack of pectin or acid, or by under-boiling so that the pectin is not fully released.

EQUIPMENT

Jam making requires little in the way of specialist equipment. The most worthwhile investment for the avid jam maker is a good-quality preserving pan. Most of the other items shown here are pieces of everyday equipment.

CITRUS FRUIT SQUEEZER

WEIGHING SCALES
The dial on the scale is either in both metric and imperial or in one measurement only.

MEASURING JUG
Plastic, china, glass, or stainless steel measuring jugs are all suitable. Other metals should be avoided, particularly if lemon juice is being used.

STAINLESS STEEL SPOON
Plain or slotted for skimming.

LADLE

SUGAR THERMOMETER

CHOPPING BOARD, SHARP STAINLESS STEEL KNIVES, AND VEGETABLE PEELER

MEASURING SPOONS

MUSLIN
For wrapping up spices or pith and pips, and for straining.

WOODEN SPOONS
Choose long-handled ones so that the hot preserve doesn't splash your hand.

DID YOU KNOW?
A wide variety of jam jars and closures are available. The most effective container for long-term storage is a glass jar with a screw-top lid, because the lid is airtight. Wax discs and cellophane circles are also useful for covering jams on a short-term basis. The wax disc is placed on the jam, wax-side down, and smoothed over with a fingertip to remove air pockets. A damp cellophane circle is then placed over the jar and secured with a rubber band. Stationers often sell packets containing sets of wax-disc equipment.

PLASTIC SIEVES
Metal sieves can give an unpleasant flavour to jam, so always use plastic ones.

LABELS

PRESERVING PAN
A wide, fairly shallow preserving pan, made of good-quality stainless steel, is best for rapid boiling of fruit and sugar. Avoid using brass or copper, unless specified in the recipe.

CONTAINERS
Use sterilized and dried jars and closures.

FUNNELS
Essential for pouring liquids from one container to another, especially bottles with narrow necks.

PLUM AND WALNUT JAM

Late summer is the time to make this jam, and plums, in all their different hues, offer a wide choice of colours. Try blending red and yellow plums to give a deep shade of pink to your pots of jam. Chopped nuts stirred in at the last minute make an interesting addition.

INGREDIENTS

1 kg (2 lb) red plums

1 kg (2 lb) yellow plums

450 ml (15 fl oz) water

1.8 kg (4 lb) sugar, warmed (see box, page 20)

225 g (8 oz) walnuts, roughly chopped

Makes about 2.75 kg (6 lb)

1 ◄ Halve and stone the plums. Crack a few of the stones with a hammer and take out the kernels. Discard the rest.

2 Put the kernels into a bowl and pour over boiling water to cover. Leave for 1 minute, then drain and transfer to a bowl of cold water. Drain again, and rub off the skins.

3 ◄ Put the plums, kernels, and measured water into a preserving pan and bring to a boil. Lower the heat and simmer, stirring occasionally, for 30–40 minutes, or until the plum skins are soft and the fruit is tender. The mixture in the pan should have reduced by about one-third.

4 ◀ Add the warmed sugar, and stir over a low heat, until the sugar has completely dissolved. Increase the heat and boil the mixture rapidly, without stirring, for 10 minutes, or until it reaches setting point. Remove the pan from the heat to test.

5 ▼ The sugar thermometer should read 104°C (220°F). If you do not have a thermometer, test for set with the cold plate test (see page 15). Lightly skim off any scum, using a long-handled metal spoon.

6 ▲ Stir in the walnuts. Immediately pour the jam into warmed sterilized jars, to within 3 mm (¹⁄₈ inch) of the tops. Seal the jars and label.

LATTICED PLUM PIE
Plum and Walnut Jam fills this luscious tart, topped with a decorative lattice of pastry.

PEACH JAM

INGREDIENTS

2 kg (4¹/₂ lb) peaches

300 ml (10 fl oz) water

1.8 kg (4 lb) sugar with pectin
(jam sugar)

When using sugar with pectin, which is available in most supermarkets, the boiling time is shorter and there is no need to test for set.

1 Halve, stone, peel, and dice the peaches. Crack a few of the stones with a hammer and take out the kernels. Discard the rest. Put the kernels into a small bowl and pour over boiling water to cover. Leave for 1 minute, then drain and transfer to a bowl of cold water. Drain again, then rub off the skins with your fingers.

2 Put the peaches, kernels, and the measured water into a preserving pan and bring to a boil. Lower the heat and simmer, stirring occasionally, for 20–30 minutes, or until the peaches are soft. Add the sugar with pectin, and stir with a wooden spoon, until the sugar has completely dissolved.

3 Increase the heat and boil the mixture rapidly, without stirring, for only 4 minutes. With the pan off the heat, lightly skim off any scum from the surface of the jam, using a long-handled metal spoon. Cool the jam slightly.

4 Pour the jam into warmed sterilized jars, to within 3 mm (¹/₈ inch) of the tops. Seal the jars and label.

Makes about 2.25 kg (5 lb)

DID YOU KNOW?
Jam will not set without pectin, a setting agent found naturally in most fruits, in varying degrees. Jams made with fruits which are low in pectin, such as peaches, are best made with a special sugar packaged with pectin added to ensure a good set.

PEAR AND DAMSON JAM

INGREDIENTS

1 kg (2 lb) Conference pears

1 kg (2 lb) damsons

300 ml (10 fl oz) water

1.8 kg (4 lb) sugar, warmed
(see box, below)

1 Halve, core, peel, and dice the pears. Put the peel and cores on a square of muslin and tie up tightly into a bag with a long piece of string. Put the diced pears, damsons, and water into a preserving pan. Tie the muslin bag to the pan handle, so that it rests on the fruit, and bring to a boil.

2 Lower the heat and simmer, stirring occasionally, for at least 1 hour, or until the damson skins are soft and the fruit is tender. The mixture in the pan should have reduced by about one-third. Skim off and discard the damson stones with a slotted spoon as they come to the surface. Discard the bag, squeezing it first to extract all the juice.

3 Add the warmed sugar to the fruit mixture, and stir over a low heat, until the sugar has completely dissolved.

4 Increase the heat and boil the mixture rapidly, without stirring, for 10 minutes, or until it reaches setting point. Continue to skim off the stones from the top. Remove the pan from the heat to test. The sugar thermometer should read 104°C (220°F). If you do not have a sugar thermometer, test for set with the cold plate test (see page 15).

5 With the pan off the heat, lightly skim off any remaining stones and any scum from the surface of the jam.

6 Immediately pour the jam into warmed sterilized jars, to within 3 mm (¹/₈ inch) of the tops. Seal the jars and label.

Makes about 2.25 kg (5 lb)

WARMING SUGAR Sugar will dissolve quickly in the fruit mixture if it is warmed first. Put the oven on its lowest setting. Weigh the sugar and put it into an ovenproof bowl. Warm the sugar in the oven for about 15 minutes. The sterilized jars can be put into the oven to warm at the same time.

CRUSHED STRAWBERRY JAM

INGREDIENTS

1.9 kg (4¼ lb) strawberries

90 ml (6 tbsp) lemon juice

*1.8 kg (4 lb) sugar, warmed
(see box, page 20)*

1 Hull the strawberries and check their weight. You should have 1.8 kg (4 lb) hulled fruit. Halve the strawberries and put into a non-metallic bowl. Lightly crush them with a potato masher.

2 Put the crushed strawberries and lemon juice into a preserving pan and bring to a boil. Lower the heat and simmer for 5–10 minutes, or until the strawberries are soft.

3 Add the warmed sugar to the strawberry mixture, and stir over a low heat, until the sugar has completely dissolved.

4 Increase the heat and boil the mixture rapidly, without stirring, for 15 minutes, or until it reaches setting point. Remove the pan from the heat to test. The sugar thermometer should read 104°C (220°F). If you do not have a sugar thermometer, test for set with the cold plate test (see page 15).

5 With the pan off the heat, lightly skim off any scum from the surface of the jam, using a long-handled metal spoon. Cool the jam slightly.

6 Pour the jam into warmed sterilized jars, to within 3 mm (⅛ inch) of the tops. Seal the jars and label.

Makes about 2.25 kg (5 lb)

WHOLE STRAWBERRY JAM Leave whole hulled strawberries to stand with the lemon juice and cold sugar overnight. Put the mixture into a preserving pan, heat gently, and continue as directed from step 4. Leave for 15 minutes before putting into jars.

BRANDIED CARROT JAM

INGREDIENTS

1 kg (2 lb) young carrots

900 ml (1½ pints) water

*675 g (1½ lb) sugar, warmed
(see box, page 20)*

*finely grated zest and juice of
2 large lemons*

*15 ml (1 tbsp) freshly grated
root ginger*

30 ml (2 tbsp) brandy

1 Top and tail, scrape, and coarsely chop the carrots. Put the carrots and water into a preserving pan and bring to a boil. Lower the heat, and simmer, covered, for 20 minutes, or until the carrots are very soft. Purée the carrots in a food processor or blender. Alternatively, press them through a plastic sieve.

2 Return the carrots to the pan. Add the warmed sugar, lemon zest and juice, and grated ginger to the carrot mixture. Stir over a low heat, until the sugar has completely dissolved.

3 Increase the heat and boil the mixture rapidly, without stirring, for 15–20 minutes, or until it reaches setting point. Remove the pan from the heat to test. The sugar thermometer should read 104°C (220°F). If you do not have a sugar thermometer, test for set with the cold plate test (see page 15).

4 With the pan off the heat, skim off any scum from the surface of the jam, using a long-handled metal spoon. Stir in the brandy.

5 Immediately pour the jam into warmed sterilized jars, to within 3 mm (⅛ inch) of the tops. Seal the jars and label.

**Makes about
575 g (1¼ lb)**

BLUEBERRY JAM

INGREDIENTS

1.8 kg (4 lb) blueberries

1.4 kg (3 lb) sugar

juice of 2 lemons

pinch of salt

Sweet spicy blueberries are a North American favourite, and are distant relatives of the European bilberry.

1 Put the blueberries into a non-metallic bowl with half of the sugar, all of the lemon juice, and the salt. Stir to mix, cover, and leave to stand for about 5 hours.

2 Pour the contents of the bowl into a preserving pan. Add the remaining sugar, and stir over a low heat, with a wooden spoon, until the sugar has completely dissolved.

3 Increase the heat and boil the mixture rapidly, without stirring, for 10–12 minutes, or until it reaches setting point. Remove the pan from the heat to test. The sugar thermometer should read 104°C (220°F). Alternatively, test for set with the cold plate test (see page 15).

4 With the pan off the heat, skim off any scum from the surface of the jam, using a long-handled metal spoon.

5 Immediately pour the jam into warmed sterilized jars, to within 3 mm (1/8 inch) of the tops. Seal the jars and label.

Makes about 3.25 kg (7 lb)

RASPBERRY AND REDCURRANT JAM

From left to right,
Blueberry Jam,
Pineapple Jam, and
Raspberry and
Redcurrant Jam

INGREDIENTS

225 g (8 oz) redcurrants

1.15 litres (2 pints) water

1.8 kg (4 lb) raspberries

2.25 kg (5 lb) sugar, warmed (see box, page 20)

1 Put the redcurrants into a preserving pan set over a low heat. When the juices start to run, add the water, and bring to a boil. Simmer, stirring, for 15 minutes.

2 Strain the redcurrants through a plastic sieve into a large measuring jug, pressing with the back of a wooden spoon to extract all the juice. Discard the pulp in the sieve. The juice should measure 900 ml (1 1/2 pints), so reduce it if necessary by boiling it for longer.

3 Pour the redcurrant juice back into the pan. Add the raspberries and return to a boil. Lower the heat and simmer for 10 minutes. Add the warmed sugar to the mixture, and stir, until the sugar has completely dissolved.

4 Increase the heat and boil the mixture rapidly, without stirring, for 10–15 minutes, or until it reaches setting point. Remove the pan from the heat to test. The sugar thermometer should read 104°C (220°F). Alternatively, test for set with the cold plate test (see page 15).

5 With the pan off the heat, lightly skim off any scum from the surface of the jam, using a long-handled metal spoon. Immediately pour the jam into warmed sterilized jars, to within 3 mm (1/8 inch) of the tops. Seal the jars and label.

Makes about 3.25 kg (7 lb)

BLACKBERRY AND APPLE JAM

INGREDIENTS

1 kg (2 lb) cooking apples

300 ml (10 fl oz) water

1.8 kg (4 lb) blackberries

2.75 kg (6 lb) sugar, warmed (see box, page 20)

1 Peel, core, and roughly chop the apples. You should have about 675 g (1 1/2 lb) in weight. Put the apples and half of the water into a medium saucepan. Bring to a boil, lower the heat, and simmer, stirring occasionally, for about 10 minutes, or until the apples are quite soft. Set aside.

2 Put the blackberries and the remaining water into a preserving pan. Bring to a boil, and simmer for about 15 minutes, or until the blackberries are soft. Add the apples and return to a boil. Add the warmed sugar to the fruit mixture, and stir with a wooden spoon until the sugar has completely dissolved.

3 Increase the heat and boil the mixture rapidly, without stirring, for about 10 minutes, or until it reaches setting point. Remove the pan from the heat to test. The sugar thermometer should read 104°C (220°F). If you do not have a sugar thermometer, test for set with the cold plate test (see page 15).

4 With the pan off the heat, lightly skim off any scum from the surface of the jam, using a long-handled metal spoon. Immediately pour the jam into warmed sterilized jars, to within 3 mm (1/8 inch) of the tops. Seal the jars and label.

Makes about 4.5 kg (10 lb)

PINEAPPLE JAM

INGREDIENTS

2 ripe pineapples, total weight about 1.4 kg (3 lb) with leaves

sugar

about 2 lemons

1 Slice the tops off the pineapples. Cut off the peel in strips, cutting deep enough to remove the "eyes" with the peel. Cut the pineapples across into thick slices, cut out and discard the hard central core from each slice; dice the flesh. Weigh the fruit. For each 450 g (1 lb) fruit, weigh 450 g (1 lb) sugar. Put the fruit into a saucepan. Warm the sugar (see box, page 20), and add it to the fruit.

2 Allow 1 lemon for each 450 g (1 lb) fruit. Peel off the zest and slice it finely. Halve and squeeze the lemons, keeping the pips and juice. Roughly chop the squeezed lemon halves. Put them with the pips on a square of muslin and tie up tightly into a bag with a long piece of string.

3 Put the lemon zest and juice into the pan with the pineapple and tie the muslin bag to the pan handle. Stir over a low heat, until the sugar has completely dissolved. Increase the heat and bring to a boil, then simmer, stirring occasionally, for about 1 1/2 hours. Remove the pan from the heat. Test for set with the cold plate test (see page 15). It will be a lighter set than most jams. Discard the bag, squeezing it first to extract all the juice.

4 With the pan off the heat, lightly skim off any scum from the surface of the jam, using a long-handled metal spoon. Immediately pour the jam into warmed sterilized jars, to within 3 mm (1/8 inch) of the tops. Seal the jars and label.

Makes about 1.4 kg (3 lb)

Nectarine Jam

INGREDIENTS

1 kg (2 lb) nectarines

240 ml (8 fl oz) water

675 g (1 1/2 lb) sugar with pectin
(jam sugar)

Nectarines, like peaches, are low in pectin, so it is easier to achieve a set with this jam if a special jam sugar, with pectin already added, is used. There is no need to add lemon juice when using jam sugar, because the sugar already contains citric acid. The jam reaches setting point quickly, in only 4 minutes.

1 Halve and stone the nectarines, but do not peel them. Chop them coarsely.

2 Put the chopped nectarines and water into a preserving pan, and simmer for 15 minutes, or until the fruit is soft.

3 Crush the chopped nectarines with a potato masher. Add the sugar to the nectarine mixture, and stir over a low heat, with a wooden spoon, until the sugar has completely dissolved.

4 Increase the heat and boil the mixture rapidly, without stirring, for only 4 minutes.

5 With the pan off the heat, lightly skim off any scum from the surface of the jam, using a long-handled metal spoon. Cool the jam slightly.

6 Pour the jam into warmed sterilized jars, to within 3 mm (1/8 inch) of the tops. Seal the jars and label.

Makes about 675 g (1 1/2 lb)

COOK'S TIP Use a small sharp knife to remove stones from fruits. Using the indentation on one side as a guide, cut the fruit in half. Then, with both hands, give a sharp twist to each half to loosen the stone. Lift or scoop out the stone with the knife.

Loganberry Jam

INGREDIENTS

2.75 kg (6 lb) loganberries

juice of 1 lemon

2.75 kg (6 lb) sugar, warmed
(see box, page 20)

1 Put the loganberries and lemon juice into a preserving pan. Simmer over a medium heat, stirring, until the juices run free. Bring the mixture to a boil, then lower the heat and simmer, stirring occasionally, for 15–20 minutes, or until the fruit is soft.

2 Add the warmed sugar to the loganberry mixture, and stir with a wooden spoon, until the sugar has completely dissolved.

3 Increase the heat and boil the mixture rapidly, without stirring, for 4–6 minutes, or until it reaches setting point. Remove the pan from the heat to test. The sugar thermometer should read 104°C (220°F). If you do not have a sugar thermometer, test for set with the cold plate test (see page 15).

4 With the pan off the heat, lightly skim off any scum from the surface of the jam, using a long-handled metal spoon.

5 Immediately pour the jam into warmed sterilized jars, to within 3 mm (1/8 inch) of the tops. Seal the jars and label.

Makes about 4.5 kg (10 lb)

VARIATIONS
Raspberries can be used in place of loganberries. Alternatively, try using dewberries, boysenberries, blackberries, even a mixture of berries. Wild or freshly picked berries give jams the best flavour.

RHUBARB AND STRAWBERRY JAM

INGREDIENTS

1.4 kg (3 lb) rhubarb

450 g (1 lb) strawberries

1.4 kg (3 lb) sugar

3 lemons

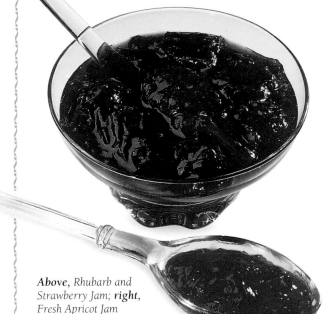

***Above**, Rhubarb and Strawberry Jam;* **right,** *Fresh Apricot Jam*

Rhubarb and strawberries combined together make a wonderfully scented chunky jam.

1 Trim the rhubarb and cut the stalks into 1.25 cm ($^1/_2$ inch) pieces. Hull and halve the strawberries. Layer the fruit pieces with the sugar in a large non-metallic bowl. Halve and squeeze the lemons, keeping the pips, juice, and lemon halves. Pour the juice over the layered fruit. Cover and leave to stand overnight, to draw out the juices.

2 Roughly chop the squeezed lemon halves. Put them with the pips on a square of muslin and tie up tightly into a bag with a long piece of string. Pour the rhubarb and strawberry mixture into a preserving pan and tie the muslin bag to the pan handle, so that it rests on the fruit.

3 Bring the mixture to a boil over a high heat and boil rapidly, without stirring, for 15 minutes, or until it reaches setting point. Remove the pan from the heat to test. The sugar thermometer should read 104°C (220°F). If you do not have a sugar thermometer, test for set with the cold plate test (see page 15). Lift the bag out of the pan and squeeze all the juice back into the pan. Discard the bag.

4 With the pan off the heat, lightly skim off any scum from the surface of the jam, using a long-handled metal spoon. Immediately pour the jam into warmed sterilized jars, to within 3 mm ($^1/_8$ inch) of the tops. Seal the jars and label.

Makes about 2 kg (4$^1/_2$ lb)

FRESH APRICOT JAM

INGREDIENTS

2.75 kg (6 lb) apricots

600 ml (1 pint) water

juice of 1 lemon

2.75 kg (6 lb) sugar, warmed (see box, page 20)

1 Halve and stone the apricots. Crack a few of the stones with a hammer and take out the kernels. Discard the rest. Put the kernels into a small bowl and pour over boiling water to cover. Leave for 1 minute, then drain and transfer to a bowl of cold water. Drain again, then rub off the skins with your fingers.

2 Put the apricots, kernels, measured water, and lemon juice into a preserving pan and bring to a boil. Lower the heat and simmer, stirring occasionally, for 20–30 minutes, or until the apricot skins are soft and the fruit is tender. The mixture in the pan should have reduced by about one-third. Add the warmed sugar to the apricot mixture and stir until the sugar has completely dissolved.

3 Increase the heat and boil, without stirring, for 10 minutes, or until it reaches setting point. Remove the pan from the heat to test. The sugar thermometer should read 104°C (220°F). Alternatively, test for set with the cold plate test (see page 15).

4 With the pan off the heat, lightly skim off any scum from the surface of the jam, using a long-handled metal spoon. Immediately pour the jam into warmed sterilized jars, to within 3 mm ($^1/_8$ inch) of the tops. Seal the jars and label.

Makes about 4.5 kg (10 lb)

BLACKCURRANT JAM

INGREDIENTS

1.8 kg (4 lb) blackcurrants

1.4 litres (2¹/₂ pints) water

*2.75 kg (6 lb) sugar, warmed
(see box, page 20)*

Blackcurrants are the ideal fruit for jam making, because they have a high level of pectin. Remove them from their stalks with a fork.

1 Put the blackcurrants and water into a preserving pan and bring to a boil. Lower the heat and simmer, stirring occasionally with a wooden spoon, for 50–60 minutes, or until the blackcurrant skins are soft and the fruit is tender. The fruit mixture should have reduced by about one-third.

2 Add the warmed sugar to the blackcurrant mixture, and stir over a low heat, until the sugar has completely dissolved.

3 Increase the heat and boil the mixture rapidly, without stirring, for 6–8 minutes, or until it reaches setting point. (This jam reaches setting point quickly, so start testing early.) Remove the pan from the heat to test. The sugar thermometer should read 104°C (220°F). If you do not have a sugar thermometer, test for set with the cold plate test (see page 15).

4 With the pan off the heat, lightly skim off any scum from the surface of the jam, using a long-handled metal spoon.

5 Immediately pour the jam into warmed sterilized jars, to within 3 mm (¹/₈ inch) of the tops. Seal the jars and label.

Makes about 3.25 kg (7 lb)

GREENGAGE JAM

INGREDIENTS

2 kg (4¹/₂ lb) greengages

450 ml (³/₄ pint) water

*1.8 kg (4 lb) sugar, warmed
(see box, page 20)*

1 Halve and stone the greengages and check their weight. You should have 1.8 kg (4 lb) stoned fruit. Crack a few of the stones with a hammer and take out the kernels. Discard the rest. Put the kernels into a small bowl and pour over boiling water to cover. Leave for 1 minute, then drain and transfer to a bowl of cold water. Drain again, then rub off the skins with your fingers.

2 Put the greengages, kernels, and measured water into a copper or brass pan and bring to a boil. Lower the heat and simmer, stirring occasionally, for 30–40 minutes, or until the greengage skins are soft and the fruit is tender. The mixture in the pan should have reduced by about one-third.

3 Add the warmed sugar to the greengage mixture, and stir over a low heat, until the sugar has completely dissolved.

4 Increase the heat and boil the mixture rapidly, without stirring, for about 10 minutes, or until it reaches setting point. Remove the pan from the heat to test. The sugar thermometer should read 104°C (220°F). If you do not have a sugar thermometer, test for set with the cold plate test (see page 15).

5 With the pan off the heat, lightly skim off any scum from the surface of the jam, using a long-handled metal spoon.

6 Immediately pour the jam into warmed sterilized jars, to within 3 mm (¹/₈ inch) of the tops. Seal the jars and label.

Makes about 2.25 kg (5 lb)

DID YOU KNOW? Jams made with greengages and gooseberries tend to discolour when made in a stainless steel pan. Use a copper or brass pan instead.

Apple and Ginger Jam

Ingredients

2.75 kg (6 lb) cooking apples

1.15 litres (2 pints) water

10 ml (2 tsp) ground ginger

finely grated zest and juice of
4 lemons

75 g (3 oz) crystallized ginger
or stem ginger in syrup

2.75 kg (6 lb) sugar, warmed
(see box, page 20)

1 Peel, core, and roughly chop the apples. Put the peel and cores on a square of muslin and tie up tightly into a bag with a long piece of string. Put the apples and water into a preserving pan with the ground ginger, lemon zest and juice. Tie the muslin bag to the pan handle. Bring to a boil, lower the heat and simmer, stirring occasionally, for 10 minutes, or until the apples are soft. Discard the bag, squeezing it first to extract all the juice.

2 Chop the crystallized or the stem ginger; set aside. Add the warmed sugar to the apples, and stir over a low heat, until the sugar has completely dissolved.

3 Increase the heat and boil the mixture rapidly, without stirring, for 10 minutes, or until it reaches setting point. Remove the pan from the heat to test. The sugar thermometer should read 104°C (220°F). If you do not have a sugar thermometer, test for set with the cold plate test (see page 15).

4 With the pan off the heat, lightly skim off any scum from the surface of the jam, using a long-handled metal spoon. Stir in the ginger, and pour the jam into warmed sterilized jars, to within 3 mm (1/8 inch) of the tops. Seal the jars and label.

Makes about 4.15 kg (9 lb)

Gooseberry and Elderflower Jam

Ingredients

1.8 kg (4 lb) gooseberries

600 ml (1 pint) water

5 large elderflowers

2.25 kg (5 lb) sugar, warmed
(see box, page 20)

1 Top and tail the gooseberries. Put them with the water into a copper or brass preserving pan (see box, page 26).

2 Cut off and discard the stems from the elderflowers, and wash the elderflower heads. Put them on a large square of muslin and tie up tightly into a bag with a long piece of string. Tie the muslin bag to the pan handle, so that it rests on the fruit, and bring the fruit and flower mixture to a boil. Lower the heat and simmer, stirring occasionally, for 30–40 minutes, or until the fruit is soft. The mixture in the pan should have reduced by about one-third. Discard the bag, squeezing it first to extract all of the juice.

3 Add the warmed sugar to the gooseberry mixture, and stir over a low heat, until the sugar has completely dissolved.

4 Increase the heat and boil the mixture rapidly, without stirring, for 6–8 minutes, or until it reaches setting point. (This jam reaches setting point quickly, so start testing early.) Remove the pan from the heat to test. The sugar thermometer should read 104°C (220°F). If you do not have a sugar thermometer, test for set with the cold plate test (see page 15).

5 With the pan off the heat, lightly skim off any scum from the surface of the jam, using a long-handled metal spoon.

6 Immediately pour the jam into warmed sterilized jars, to within 3 mm (1/8 inch) of the tops. Seal the jars and label.

Makes about 3.25 kg (7 lb)

PRESERVES & CONSERVES

FRUIT PRESERVES, in the narrow sense of the word, are whole fruits or pieces of fruit preserved in a thick syrup – a definition that is accurate but cannot possibly convey the deliciousness of biting into fruits captured from summer by the subtle use of sugar.

Almost any fruits can be preserved for our enjoyment in this very simple way – peaches, pears, and strawberries are suitable, so too are exotics like melons and kiwi fruit. You can preserve each type of fruit on its own, or mix several different ones together for extra flavour and interest. Serve preserves by themselves, as a dessert topping with ice cream, or on a sponge flan base topped with fresh fruit and whipped cream.

A close culinary cousin of the preserve is the conserve, best described as a type of jam. Conserves are often made with two or more fruits, one of which may be a citrus fruit, and usually raisins or nuts are added. They were eaten on their own as a dessert course in Victorian and Edwardian days, but these days they are more usually served as spreads, like jams and jellies, or as dessert sauces. They also make fine accompaniments to savoury dishes.

MAKING PRESERVES & CONSERVES

❧ Choose the ingredients. All fresh fruits should be picked or purchased when slightly under-ripe. Dried fruits – prunes, raisins, and apricots – can also be used, provided that they have not been preserved with sulphur dioxide, because this affects the set. Any dried fruits should be soaked overnight before using in these recipes.

❧ Prepare the fruits. Pick over soft fruits, removing and discarding any mouldy or damaged parts. Cut out any blemishes from firmer fruits, such as pears. Wash the fruits, using as little cold water as possible for soft fruits. Pat the fruits dry on kitchen paper to remove all excess water. Stone fruits should be halved and stoned, and a few kernels reserved if the recipe calls for it.

❧ For preserves, the chosen fruit is layered with sugar in a non-metallic bowl and left to stand overnight. This helps toughen the fruit, enabling it to stay whole, and it also draws out the juices. The next day, the fruit, sugar, and extracted juices are boiled together briefly until a thick syrup is formed. Cool until the fruit remains suspended in the syrup.

❧ The method of making conserves is very similar to jams but they have a shorter cooking time, so they retain their natural flavour better. The fruit is cooked over a low heat until the sugar completely dissolves, and then boiled fast to reach a light set.

❧ To test for a light set, drop a little mixture on a cold plate and chill quickly; if the conserve forms a slight wrinkle when pushed with a finger, it is ready.

❧ If adding nuts or alcohol, such as blanched or flaked almonds or Grand Marnier, then add them at the last minute, because cooking them will destroy their flavour. Pour the preserves or conserves into warmed sterilized jars (see page 11).

How to seal and store

Seal the preserve or conserve as soon as it has been put into the jar. Choose screw-top lids with plastic linings that can be secured tightly. Label the jars. Preserves and conserves do not keep as long as jam, and should be eaten within 3 months. To keep them longer, store them in the refrigerator. They should then last about 6 months.

What can go wrong and why

If the fruit does not stay whole in a preserve, it has not been left overnight with the sugar, or it has been cooked too long. If the preserve or conserve shrinks in the jar, the seal is faulty or the storage conditions are too warm. Air pockets in the jar are caused if the preserve or conserve is too cool before being poured into the jar. Problems that occur in jams also apply to these recipes (see page 15).

PRUNE CONSERVE

INGREDIENTS

675 g (1 1/2 lb) prunes

675 g (1 1/2 lb) raisins

675 g (1 1/2 lb) currants

1.15 litres (2 pints) hot strong tea

450 g (1 lb) dark brown muscovado sugar

3–5 whole cloves

juice of 1 lemon

100 g (4 oz) whole blanched almonds

100 ml (4 fl oz) brandy or kirsch

1 Stone the prunes and chop them roughly. Crack a few of the stones with a hammer and take out the kernels. Discard the rest.

2 Put the kernels into a small bowl and pour over boiling water to cover. Leave for 1 minute, then drain and transfer to a bowl of cold water. Drain again, then rub off the skins with your fingers.

3 Put the chopped prunes and peeled kernels into a non-metallic bowl with the raisins and currants. Pour the hot tea over the fruit. Cover and leave to stand overnight.

4 Pour the contents of the bowl into a preserving pan. Stir in all the remaining ingredients, except the almonds, brandy or kirsch, and put the pan over a low heat. Stir with a wooden spoon until the sugar has completely dissolved.

5 Bring the mixture to a boil. Simmer, stirring constantly, for 12 minutes, or until the mixture has thickened. Remove the pan from the heat. Test for a light set (see page 28). Stir in the whole almonds and brandy or kirsch.

6 Pour the conserve into warmed sterilized jars, to within 3 mm (1/8 inch) of the tops. Seal the jars and label.

Makes about 3.25 kg (7 lb)

PEACH AND MELON PRESERVE

INGREDIENTS

1.15 kg (2 1/2 lb) peaches

1.4 kg (3 lb) melon

1.4 kg (3 lb) sugar

50 ml (2 fl oz) lemon juice

pinch of ground ginger

100 g (4 oz) whole blanched almonds

1 Stone, peel, and roughly chop the peaches. Peel, seed, and chop the melon into large chunks. You should have 1 kg (2 lb) each of chopped peaches and melon.

2 Layer the fruits with the sugar in a large non-metallic bowl. Cover and leave to stand overnight.

3 Pour the contents of the bowl into a preserving pan and add the lemon juice and ground ginger. Stir the mixture over a low heat until the sugar has completely dissolved.

4 Increase the heat and boil the mixture rapidly for 20 minutes, or until the mixture has thickened.

5 Remove the pan from the heat and cool slightly until the fruit remains suspended in the syrup. Coarsely chop the almonds and gently stir into the mixture. Pour the preserve into warmed sterilized jars, to within 3 mm (1/8 inch) of the tops. Seal the jars and label.

Makes about 2.75 kg (6 lb)

*Above, Peach and Melon Preserve; **above right**, Prune Conserve*

STRAWBERRY PRESERVE

INGREDIENTS

1.8 kg (4 lb) small strawberries

1.8 kg (4 lb) sugar

juice of 1 lemon

Here, whole strawberries are suspended in a sugar syrup.

1 Hull the strawberries. Layer them with the sugar in a non-metallic bowl. Cover and leave to stand overnight.

2 Pour the contents of the bowl into a preserving pan and add the lemon juice. Bring the mixture to a boil, and simmer for 5 minutes. Return the strawberry mixture to the bowl, cover, and leave for 24 hours.

3 Return the strawberry mixture to the pan and boil rapidly for 20–25 minutes, or until the syrup has thickened. Cool slightly until the strawberries remain suspended in the syrup. Pour the preserve into warmed sterilized jars, to within 3 mm ($^{1}/_{8}$ inch) of the tops. Seal the jars and label.

COOK'S TIP Strawberry Preserve can be used to make strawberry pavlova – spread a layer of the preserve carefully in a baked meringue shell, and top with whipped cream and fresh strawberries.

Makes about 2.25 kg (5 lb)

DRIED APRICOT CONSERVE

INGREDIENTS

1 kg (2 lb) dried apricots

2.25 litres (4 pints) water

juice of 2 lemons

1.8 kg (4 lb) sugar, warmed (see box, page 36)

175 g (6 oz) blanched almonds

1 Coarsely chop the apricots. Put them into a non-metallic bowl with the water. Cover and leave to stand overnight.

2 Pour the contents of the bowl into a preserving pan and add the lemon juice. Bring to a boil, and simmer for 15–20 minutes, or until the apricots are really soft. Add the warmed sugar. Stir the mixture over a low heat, with a wooden spoon, until the sugar has completely dissolved.

3 Boil the mixture rapidly, without stirring, for 10–12 minutes, or until it has thickened. Remove the pan from the heat to test. Test for a light set (see page 28). Stir in the blanched almonds and cool slightly.

4 Pour the conserve into warmed sterilized jars, to within 3 mm ($^{1}/_{8}$ inch) of the tops. Seal the jars and label.

Makes about 3.25 kg (7 lb)

GOOSEBERRY AND ALMOND CONSERVE

INGREDIENTS

1 kg (2 lb) gooseberries

175 ml (6 fl oz) lemon juice

300 ml (10 fl oz) water

1 kg (2 lb) sugar, warmed (see box, page 36)

100 g (4 oz) flaked almonds

1 Top and tail the gooseberries.

2 Combine the gooseberries, lemon juice, and water in a copper or brass pan (see box, page 26). Add the warmed sugar, and stir over a low heat, until the sugar has completely dissolved.

3 Boil the mixture rapidly, stirring occasionally, for 15–20 minutes, or until it has thickened. Remove the pan from the heat to test. Test for a light set (see page 28). Stir in the flaked almonds and cool slightly.

4 Pour the conserve into warmed sterilized jars, to within 3 mm ($^{1}/_{8}$ inch) of the tops. Seal the jars and label.

Makes about 1.4 kg (3 lb)

MELON AND ORANGE PRESERVE

INGREDIENTS

2.1 kg (4³/₄ lb) melon

775 g (1³/₄ lb) sugar

finely grated zest and juice of 1 large orange

juice of 1 lemon

1 Peel and seed the melon, cut into 1.25 cm (¹/₂ inch) cubes, and check the weight. You should have 1.4 kg (3 lb) melon flesh. Layer the melon with the sugar in a non-metallic bowl. Cover and leave to stand overnight.

2 Pour the contents of the bowl into a preserving pan and add the grated orange zest and the orange and lemon juice.

3 Bring the mixture to a boil over a high heat, and boil rapidly for 20–25 minutes, or until the syrup has reduced. Cool slightly until the melon remains suspended in the syrup.

4 Pour the preserve into warmed sterilized jars, to within 3 mm (¹/₈ inch) of the tops. Seal the jars and label.

Makes about 1.4 kg (3 lb)

PEAR AND CASHEW CONSERVE

INGREDIENTS

1 kg (2 lb) pears

300 ml (10 fl oz) water

juice of 1 lemon

1.15 kg (2¹/₂ lb) sugar, warmed (see box, page 36)

75 g (3 oz) cashew nuts

1 Peel, halve, and core the pears, and cut the flesh into cubes. Put the pears into a saucepan with the water and lemon juice. Bring to boil and simmer for 10 minutes, or until the pears are soft and tender.

2 Add the warmed sugar to the fruit mixture and stir over a low heat until the sugar has completely dissolved. Boil rapidly for 15–20 minutes, or until the mixture has thickened. Remove the pan from the heat. Test for a light set (see page 28). Chop the cashews and stir them into the conserve. Cool slightly.

3 Pour the conserve into warmed sterilized jars, to within 3 mm (¹/₈ inch) of the tops. Seal the jars and label.

Makes about 1.4 kg (3 lb)

VARIATION
Omit the cashew nuts. Add 15 ml (1 tbsp) freshly grated root ginger to the pears in the pan in step 1. When the pear preserve is cool, stir in 15 ml (1 tbsp) rum.

PLUM AND ORANGE CONSERVE

INGREDIENTS

1.4 kg (3 lb) yellow plums

100 g (4 oz) stem ginger in syrup, drained

100 g (4 oz) walnuts

300 ml (10 fl oz) water

finely grated zest and juice of 2 large oranges and 2 lemons

1.8 kg (4 lb) sugar, warmed (see box, page 36)

450 g (1 lb) raisins

30 ml (2 tbsp) brandy

1 Halve and stone the plums. Coarsely chop the drained stem ginger and the walnuts; set them aside separately.

2 Put the plum halves into a preserving pan with the water and the zest and juice of the oranges and lemons. Bring to a boil, and simmer for 30 minutes.

3 Add the warmed sugar to the fruit mixture, and stir over a low heat until the sugar has completely dissolved. Add the chopped ginger and the raisins, and return to a boil.

4 Boil rapidly until the mixture has thickened. Remove the pan from the heat. Test for a light set (see page 28). Stir in the walnuts and brandy. Cool slightly.

5 Pour the conserve into warmed sterilized jars, to within 3 mm (¹/₈ inch) of the tops. Seal the jars and label.

Makes about 3.5 kg (8 lb)

MARMALADES

IN VICTORIAN and Edwardian England, marmalade was a fruit purée that was eaten with a spoon out of an elegant small dish, and it still is served in this way in some parts of the world, including Latin America and France. But to us, marmalade is the delectable, golden wonder we make from citrus fruits and serve on toast at breakfast time.

This preserve is beautiful to look at in jars, and just about any citrus fruit can be used to make it. Marmalade can be dark coloured, thick, and chunky, or a translucent lemon jelly with thin slices of fruit. In fact, with so many possible combinations of fruit, it can be anything in between.

A citrus preserve is not just for spreading on toast. It can be mixed into puddings and cakes, or melted and used with a little liqueur to make a marmalade sauce. In Scotland, marmalade is spread on scones and oatcakes, as well as being eaten with certain meats. Make lots and keep storecupboards well stocked, because marmalade keeps exceedingly well.

MAKING MARMALADES

❧ Select the ingredients. Bitter Seville oranges give the tangiest, clearest marmalade, but their season of availability is quite short, between December and February. They can be frozen until required, but are best used within a few months, because freezing can cause their pectin level to drop slightly. Sweet oranges can also be used, but they tend to make a cloudier preserve, and are best used in combination with other fruits, such as limes, lemons, or grapefruit. Granulated sugar is the recommended sweetener. Sometimes the exact amount of sugar is not calculated until after the fruits have been cooked, so make sure you have plenty in stock before you start.

❧ Prepare the fruits. Some citrus fruits have a wax coating which should be removed by pouring boiling water over the fruits, scrubbing, and drying them. The way the fruits are prepared depends on the type of marmalade you are making. There are two basic types – jelly-like, or thick and chunky. Either slice the peel or zest by hand, or speed the job up by using a food processor, though this does not give such an even cut. Most of the pectin in citrus fruits, which is needed to set the marmalade, is found in the pith and pips. They should be tied up in a muslin bag and cooked with the rest of the ingredients.

❧ Put the sliced peel or zest, juice, specified amount of water, lemon juice if required, and muslin bag into a preserving pan and simmer for 1 hour or more, until the liquid is reduced by about one-third. This is to soften the peel thoroughly, and to extract all of the pectin. Remove the muslin bag, squeezing it out well to extract all the excess liquid.

❧ Add warmed sugar (see box, page 36), and stir until dissolved. Boil rapidly until setting point is reached. Test for set and skim (see box, page 38). Allow the marmalade to stand for a few minutes off the heat. This helps to ensure that the peel is evenly distributed throughout. As soon as a thin skin forms on the surface, stir the marmalade once, and then pour into warmed sterilized jars (see page 11).

How to seal and store
Seal the marmalade as for jams (see page 15), putting the lids on when the marmalade is cold. Label the jars. The marmalade can be used immediately, or it will keep in a cool dark place for up to 1 year.

What can go wrong and why
If the peel is tough, it has been shredded too coarsely, or cooked for too short a time before the sugar is added. If the peel rises to the surface, the jars were too hot when the marmalade was poured into them.

SEVILLE ORANGE MARMALADE

INGREDIENTS

1 kg (2 lb) Seville oranges

1 large lemon

2.25 litres (4 pints) water

*1.8 kg (4 lb) sugar, warmed
(see box, page 36)*

SEVILLE ORANGES The bitter flavour of Seville oranges makes them one of the best citrus fruits for making marmalade. Unfortunately, they are only available for a limited period, but this recipe, or any other specifying Seville oranges, can be made all year round by substituting sweet oranges for Seville. Just follow this simple formula – for each 450 g (1 lb) Seville oranges called for, weigh the same amount of sweet oranges. Remove one of the oranges and replace with 1 lemon. The lemon should be dealt with in the same way as the oranges.

1 Cut all the fruit in half and squeeze out the juice, removing and keeping the pips and any excess pith. Strain the juice into a preserving pan. Cut the orange halves in half again and slice thinly across their length. Put the sliced orange peel into the preserving pan.

2 Roughly chop the lemon halves. Put the pips, pith, and chopped lemon halves on a square of muslin and tie up tightly into a bag with a long piece of string. Tie the muslin bag to the pan handle, so that it rests on the fruit.

3 Pour in the water and bring to a boil. Simmer, stirring occasionally, for at least 2 hours, or until the peel is very soft. The mixture should have reduced by about one-third.

4 Lift the bag out of the pan and squeeze all the juice back into the pan; discard the bag. Add the warmed sugar and stir over a low heat until it has completely dissolved.

5 Increase the heat and boil rapidly, without stirring, for 15–20 minutes, or until the marmalade reaches setting point. Test for set and skim off any scum (see box, page 38).

6 Pour the marmalade into warmed sterilized jars, to within 3 mm (1/8 inch) of the tops. Seal and label.

Makes about 3.5 kg (8 lb)

MORE MARMALADE FLAVOURS

The popularity of Seville Orange Marmalade makes it a good basic recipe that can be varied by adding other flavourings. Here are a few suggestions.

Liqueur Marmalade
A few tablespoons of rum, brandy, or whisky added to marmalade turn it into a luxurious breakfast preserve. Simply follow the basic recipe above, then stir in the spirit after skimming the marmalade. Allow 30 ml (2 tbsp) spirit for each 450 g (1 lb) marmalade. Let the marmalade stand for a few minutes to ensure the orange peel is evenly distributed throughout. Stir the marmalade once, and continue as directed.

Dark Chunky Marmalade
Follow the basic recipe above, coarsely chopping the orange peel instead of thinly slicing it. When adding the sugar, also stir in 30 ml (2 tbsp) black treacle or molasses.

Seville Orange Marmalade with Almonds
Add 100 g (4 oz) flaked almonds to the basic recipe, after skimming the marmalade. Allow the marmalade to stand for a few minutes to ensure the orange peel and nuts are evenly distributed throughout. Stir the marmalade once, and continue as directed.

Brown Sugar Marmalade
For a dark colour and rich flavour, substitute 1.4 kg (3 lb) light soft brown sugar for the sugar in the basic recipe.

DID YOU KNOW?
Marmalade has a long history. Its origin stems from the Middle Ages, when it was made with quinces cooked in honey, wine, and spices, and called "marmelade". The word is derived from *marmelada,* Portuguese for quince. It was during the seventeenth century that recipes for a kind of orange marmalade appeared.

THREE-FRUIT MARMALADE

Wonderfully tangy, this marmalade can be made all year round because it does not need seasonal Seville oranges. Don't save it just for breakfast – try using it as a glossy glaze for brushing over duck, gammon rashers, and chicken breasts.

INGREDIENTS

2 grapefruit

2 large oranges

4 lemons

3.5 litres (6 pints) water

2.75 kg (6 lb) sugar, warmed (see box, page 36)

Makes about 4.75 kg (10 ½ lb)

1 ◀ Cut all of the fruit in half and squeeze out the juice. Strain the juice into a preserving pan. Remove the pips and pulp from the skins and put them on a square of muslin. Tie up tightly into a bag with a long piece of string.

2 ▶ Cut the orange and lemon halves in half again and slice thinly across their length. Cut each grapefruit half into 4 pieces and slice in the same way. Put all the sliced fruit peel into the pan.

3 ◀ Tie the muslin bag to the pan handle, so that it rests on top of the fruit peel. Pour in the water and bring to a boil. Lower the heat and simmer, stirring occasionally, for 30–40 minutes, or until the fruit peel is very soft. The mixture should have reduced by about one-third.

4 ◄ Lift the bag out of the pan and squeeze all the juice back into pan. Discard the bag. Add the warmed sugar and stir over a low heat, with a wooden spoon, until the sugar has completely dissolved.

5 ▲ Increase the heat and boil the mixture rapidly, without stirring, for 20–25 minutes, or until it reaches setting point. Remove from the heat to test. The sugar thermometer should read 104°C (220°F). Alternatively, test for set with the cold plate test (see box, below).

COLD PLATE TEST
Also known as the saucer test. Put a small spoonful of marmalade on a cold plate and chill quickly in the refrigerator. If the marmalade has boiled sufficiently, a thin skin will form on the surface and it should wrinkle when pushed with a finger. It is now at setting point.

6 ▲ With the pan off the heat, skim off any scum. Leave to cool for a few minutes until a very thin skin forms. This helps to ensure that the peel is evenly distributed.

7 Pour the marmalade into warmed sterilized jars, to within 3 mm (⅛ inch) of the tops. Seal the jars and label.

BREAKFAST TREAT
Start the day with the refreshing taste of homemade marmalade.

FINE SHRED MARMALADE

INGREDIENTS

1 kg (2 lb) Seville oranges

1 lemon

2.5 litres (4¹/₂ pints) water

sugar

WARMING SUGAR In some recipes, the amount of sugar required is calculated according to the amount of strained juice you have after the fruit is cooked. It is therefore difficult to be specific with an exact amount of sugar in the ingredients list, so make sure you have a good supply before you start. After weighing out the sugar, it can be warmed so that it dissolves more quickly in the juice. Put the oven on its lowest setting, and put the sugar in an ovenproof bowl. Warm the sugar in the oven for about 15 minutes.

1 Pare the zest from the oranges and lemon and slice it into thin strips. Put the sliced zest into a stainless steel pan with 300 ml (10 fl oz) of the water, making sure the zest is covered, and bring to a boil. Simmer, stirring occasionally, for 1 hour, or until the zest is very soft. Drain and reserve both zest and water.

2 Chop the fruit and put into a preserving pan with all the pips and the remaining 2.25 litres (4 pints) water. Bring to a boil and simmer, stirring occasionally, for about 1 hour. The mixture should have reduced by about one-third. Add the water reserved from cooking the zest.

3 Strain the pulp through a scalded jelly bag (see box, page 41). (For a clear marmalade, allow the juice to drip through without pressing it.) Measure the strained juice. For each 600 ml (1 pint) juice, weigh 450 g (1 lb) sugar. Warm the sugar (see box, left). Pour the juice into the pan, add the sugar, and stir over a low heat until the sugar has completely dissolved.

4 Add the reserved zest and bring to a boil. Boil rapidly, without stirring, for 10–12 minutes, or until the marmalade reaches setting point. Test for set and skim off any scum (see box, page 38). Pour the marmalade into warmed sterilized jars, to within 3 mm (¹/₈ inch) of the tops. Seal the jars and label.

Makes about 2.75 kg (6 lb)

TANGERINE MARMALADE

INGREDIENTS

1 kg (2 lb) tangerines

1 grapefruit

2 lemons

3 litres (5 pints) water

1.6 kg (3¹/₂ lb) sugar, warmed (see box, above)

1 Peel the tangerines and slice the peel into thin strips. Put the strips of peel on a square of muslin and tie up tightly into a bag with a long piece of string. Chop the tangerine flesh, removing and keeping the pips. Put the flesh into a preserving pan.

2 Pare the zest from the grapefruit and lemons and slice it into thin strips, removing and keeping any excess pith. Chop the grapefruit and lemon flesh, removing and keeping the pips. Put the zest and chopped flesh into the pan. Put all the pips and pith on a square of muslin and tie up tightly into a bag with a long piece of string. Tie both muslin bags to the pan handle, so that they rest on the fruit.

3 Pour in the water and bring to a boil. Simmer, stirring occasionally, for 45 minutes, or until the zest is very soft. The mixture should have reduced by about one-third. Lift the bag of pips and pith out of the pan and squeeze all the juice back into the pan; discard the bag. Lift out the bag of tangerine peel and empty it into the pan. Add the warmed sugar and stir over a low heat until it has completely dissolved.

4 Increase the heat and boil rapidly, without stirring, for 15–20 minutes, or until the marmalade reaches setting point. Test for set and skim off any scum (see box, page 38). Pour the marmalade into warmed sterilized jars, to within 3 mm (¹/₈ inch) of the tops. Seal the jars and label.

Makes about 2.75 kg (6 lb)

PINK GRAPEFRUIT MARMALADE

INGREDIENTS

2 lemons

2 pink grapefruit

2.25 litres (4 pints) water

*1.8 kg (4 lb) sugar, warmed
(see box, page 36)*

1 Pare the zest from the lemons and slice it into thin strips. Put the sliced zest into a preserving pan. Cut the lemons and grapefruit in half and squeeze out the juice, removing and keeping the pips. Add the juice to the lemon zest in the pan.

2 Roughly chop the lemon halves and put with the pips on a square of muslin. Tie up tightly into a bag with a long piece of string. Cut the grapefruit halves into 4 pieces and slice thinly across their length. Add to the pan. Tie the muslin bag to the pan handle, so that it rests on the fruit.

3 Pour in the water and bring to a boil. Lower the heat and simmer, stirring occasionally, for 45 minutes, or until the skins are soft. The mixture should have reduced by about one-third.

4 Lift the bag out of the pan and squeeze all the juice back into the pan. Discard the bag. Add the warmed sugar and stir over a low heat until it has completely dissolved. Increase the heat and boil rapidly, without stirring, for 10–12 minutes, or until the marmalade reaches setting point. Test for set and skim off any scum (see box, page 38). Pour the marmalade into warmed sterilized jars, to within 3 mm (1/8 inch) of the tops. Seal the jars and label.

Makes about 2.25 kg (5 lb)

LEMON AND LIME MARMALADE

INGREDIENTS

4 medium lemons

4 limes

*2.25 litres
(4 pints) water*

*1.8 kg (4 lb) sugar, warmed
(see box, page 36)*

1 Pare the zest from the lemons and slice it into thin strips. Cut the pith off the lemons, roughly chop it, and set aside. Roughly chop the flesh, keeping the pips and any juice.

2 Cut the limes in half and squeeze out the juice, removing and keeping the pips and excess pith. Cut the lime halves in half again and slice thinly across their length.

3 Put all the pips and pith on a square of muslin and tie up tightly into a bag with a long piece of string.

4 Put all the fruit flesh, juice, sliced lime peel, and lemon zest into a preserving pan. Tie the muslin bag to the pan handle, so that it rests on the fruit. Pour in the water and bring to a boil. Simmer, stirring occasionally, for 1 1/2 hours, or until the skins are very soft. The mixture should have reduced by about one-third.

5 Lift the bag out of the pan and squeeze all the juice back into the pan. Discard the bag. Add the warmed sugar and stir over a low heat until it has completely dissolved. Increase the heat and boil rapidly, without stirring, for 8–10 minutes, or until the marmalade reaches setting point. Test for set and skim off any scum (see box, page 38). Pour the marmalade into warmed sterilized jars, to within 3 mm (1/8 inch) of the tops. Seal the jars and label.

*Front, Pink Grapefruit Marmalade; **back,** Lemon and Lime Marmalade*

Makes about 2.75 kg (6 lb)

Sweet Orange Marmalade

INGREDIENTS

1 kg (2 lb) sweet oranges

2 Seville oranges

1 lemon

2.25 litres (4 pints) water

1.8 kg (4 lb) sugar, warmed
(see box, page 36)

This marmalade blends sweet oranges with the more tart Seville oranges, to give a delicious and refreshing taste.

1 Cut all the fruit in half and squeeze out the juice, removing and keeping the pips and any excess pith. Pour the juice into a preserving pan. Put the pips and pith on a square of muslin and tie up tightly into a bag with a long piece of string.

2 Cut the orange halves in half again and slice them thinly across their length. Discard the lemon peel.

3 Put all the sliced peel into the pan. Tie the muslin bag to the pan handle, so that it rests on the fruit. Pour in the water and bring to a boil. Simmer, stirring occasionally, for 1½–2 hours, or until the skins are very soft. The mixture should have reduced by about one-third.

4 Lift the bag out of the pan and squeeze all the juice back into the pan. Discard the bag.

5 Add the warmed sugar and stir over a low heat until it has completely dissolved.

6 Increase the heat and boil rapidly, without stirring, for 15–20 minutes, or until the marmalade reaches setting point. Test for set and skim off any scum (see box, left). Pour the marmalade into warmed sterilized jars, to within 3 mm (⅛ inch) of the tops. Seal the jars and label.

Makes about 3.25 kg (7 lb)

TESTING FOR SET AND SKIMMING MARMALADES
Remove the pan from the heat. If using a sugar thermometer, it should read 104° C (220° F). If you do not have a thermometer, use the cold plate test: drop a little of the marmalade on a cold plate and chill quickly in the refrigerator. If it forms a skin and wrinkles when pushed with a finger, it should be ready. Lightly skim off any scum from the pan of marmalade, then leave to cool for a few minutes until a very thin skin forms. This helps to ensure that the peel is evenly distributed through the marmalade.

Quick Chunky Marmalade

INGREDIENTS

6 Seville oranges

2 large sweet oranges

2 large lemons

3.5 litres (6 pints) water

2.75 kg (6 lb) sugar, warmed
(see box, page 36)

1 Cut all the fruit in half and squeeze out the juice, removing and keeping the pips and any excess pith. Pour the juice into a preserving pan. Put the pips and pith on a square of muslin and tie up tightly into a bag with a long piece of string.

2 Cut the orange and lemon halves into smaller pieces and chop well in small batches, in a food processor, adding a little of the water, if necessary.

3 Put all the processed fruit into the pan. Tie the muslin bag to the pan handle, so that it rests on the fruit. Pour in the water and bring to a boil. Simmer, stirring occasionally, for 1½–2 hours, or until the skins are very soft. The mixture should have reduced by about one-third.

4 Lift the bag out of the pan and squeeze all the juice back into the pan. Discard the bag. Add the warmed sugar to the mixture and stir over a low heat until it has completely dissolved. Increase the heat and boil rapidly, without stirring, for 15 minutes, or until it reaches setting point. Test for set and skim off any scum (see box, above). Pour the marmalade into warmed sterilized jars, to within 3 mm (⅛ inch) of the tops. Seal the jars and label.

Makes about 3.8 kg (8½ lb)

COOK'S TIP
Chopping citrus fruits in a food processor is much quicker than by hand – although it does give a coarser cut. A blender can also be used for chopping, but the result is more like a paste.

LEMON MARMALADE

INGREDIENTS

9 large lemons

3.5 litres (6 pints) water

sugar

1 Pare the zest from the lemons, and slice it into thin strips. Roughly chop the flesh, keeping the pips and any juice. Put the pips on a square of muslin and tie up tightly into a bag with a long piece of string.

2 Put the chopped flesh, and any juice, with the sliced zest in a preserving pan. Tie the muslin bag to the pan handle, so that it rests on the fruit. Pour in the water and bring to a boil. Lower the heat and simmer, stirring occasionally, for $1-1^{1}/_{2}$ hours, or until the zest is very soft. The mixture should have reduced by about one-third.

3 Lift the bag out of the pan and squeeze all the juice back into the pan. Discard the bag. Measure the juice. For each 600 ml (1 pint) juice, weigh 450 g (1 lb) sugar. Warm the sugar (see box, page 36). Pour the juice back into the pan, add the sugar, and stir over a low heat until it has completely dissolved. Boil rapidly, without stirring, for 15 minutes, or until it reaches setting point. Test for set and skim off any scum (see box, page 38). Pour the marmalade into warmed sterilized jars, to within 3 mm ($^{1}/_{8}$ inch) of the tops. Seal the jars and label.

Makes about 2.75 kg (6 lb)

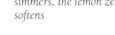

As Lemon Marmalade simmers, the lemon zest softens

GRAPEFRUIT AND GINGER MARMALADE

INGREDIENTS

3 large grapefruit

3 lemons

3.5 litres (6 pints) water

2.5 cm (1 inch) piece of fresh root ginger

2.25 kg (5 lb) sugar, warmed (see box, page 36)

175 g (6 oz) chopped crystallized ginger

1 Peel the grapefruit and lemons. Finely slice the grapefruit peel and put it into a preserving pan. Chop the flesh and add to the pan. Chop the lemon peel and put it on a square of muslin, together with the pips. Tie up tightly into a bag with a long piece of string. Tie the bag to the pan handle, so that it rests on the fruit. Add the water. Peel the root ginger, and add to the pan.

2 Bring to a boil and simmer, stirring occasionally, for $1^{1}/_{2}$ hours, or until the skins are very soft. The mixture should have reduced by about one-third.

3 Remove and discard the ginger. Lift the bag out of the pan and squeeze all the juice back into the pan. Discard the bag. Add the warmed sugar to the mixture and stir over a low heat until the sugar has completely dissolved.

4 Increase the heat and boil rapidly, without stirring, for 15 minutes, or until the marmalade reaches setting point. Test for set and skim off any scum (see box, page 38). Stir in the crystallized ginger. Pour the marmalade into warmed sterilized jars, to within 3 mm ($^{1}/_{8}$ inch) of the tops. Seal the jars and label.

Makes about 3.5 kg (8 lb)

JELLIES

BRIGHTLY COLOURED, delicately flavoured, firm yet quivering gently when released from its jar, the ideal jelly is a thing of beauty and a joy to eat. It is wonderful on toast, bread and butter, and scones, and in peanut butter sandwiches. It also makes a deliciously sweet counterpoint to savoury foods, such as poultry, pork, and game. And unlike poor Meg's jelly in Louisa May Alcott's book, *Little Women*, today's jellies do jell if the simple rules for making them are respected.

Jellies are a marvellous challenge to the imaginative cook. Peaches, cherries, and cranberries are just a few of the suitable fruits. Apples, with their high levels of pectin which help achieve set, make wonderful companions for other fruits. Apple and Orange Jelly and Apple and Chilli Jelly both testify to the versatility of the apple when making jellies. The addition of a few rose or geranium leaves can lift jellies out of the ordinary, and herbs and spices can also play an interesting role. The possibilities are infinite.

MAKING JELLIES

❧ Choose your ingredients. Select ripe fruits, but not over-ripe, with a high pectin content. Apples (including crab apples), currants, berries, and citrus fruits all make good jellies. Granulated sugar is the recommended sweetener. Make sure you have plenty of sugar in stock, because the exact amount required is not calculated until after the fruits have been cooked.

❧ Prepare the fruits. Pick over soft fruits, removing and discarding any mouldy or damaged parts. Wash and dry the fruits. Any peel, pips, and cores all go in the preserving pan with the flesh. Add water, and simmer until the fruits are soft and pulpy.

❧ Strain the pulp through a scalded jelly bag (see box, page 41). Timing varies, depending on the fruits used. Leave to strain for a few hours or overnight, but for not more than 24 hours or the fruit will start to oxidize.

❧ Measure the juice and pour into a clean preserving pan with the sugar. The amount of sugar used will depend upon the pectin content of the juice, but in general, 450 g (1 lb) sugar is required for each 600 ml (1 pint) juice. Warm the sugar before adding it to the preserving pan (see box, page 44). Stir over a low heat until the sugar has completely dissolved. Boil rapidly for 10 minutes, or until setting point is reached. As the jelly comes up to setting point, lower the heat slightly to reduce the number of bubbles. Remove the pan from the heat to test. Test for set and skim off any scum (see box, page 46).

❧ Pour the jelly into warmed sterilized jars (see page 11). Tilt the jar and pour the jelly down the side of the jar to eliminate air pockets. Work as quickly as possible, because the jelly may start to set in the pan and this will spoil the consistency of the finished jelly.

How to seal and store
Seal and store the jellies in the same way as for jams (see page 15). Do not move jar of jelly until it is completely cold and set.

What can go wrong and why
If the jelly remains runny after it is cold, it can be returned to the pan for further boiling. Jellies will be cloudy if the fruits are not clean, if the jelly bag has too coarse a mesh, or if the bag is squeezed during straining. Air pockets will form in the jelly if it is too cool before it is poured into the jars, or if it is poured into the jars too slowly. Problems that affect jams also apply to jellies (see page 15).

RED FRUIT JELLY WITH PORT

INGREDIENTS

1 kg (2 lb) redcurrants

1 kg (2 lb) raspberries

450 ml (15 fl oz) water

sugar

60 ml (4 tbsp) port

USING A JELLY BAG Jelly bags need to be supported while the juice is straining. One way of doing this is to thread a broom handle through the straps of the jelly bag, then rest each end of the broom on a chair. Place a large non-metallic bowl underneath before filling the jelly bag and leave the juice to drip undisturbed. Resist the temptation to accelerate the process by squeezing the bag, because this will result in a cloudy jelly. Leave to drip until there is only a little liquid dripping from the bag.

1 Put the redcurrants and raspberries into a preserving pan with the water. Bring to a boil, and simmer for 15–20 minutes, or until the fruits are very soft and pulpy.

2 While the fruits are cooking, prepare the jelly bag for straining the fruits. Scald it by evenly pouring through boiling water, squeeze it well, then use as directed (see box, left). Pour the fruit pulp into the jelly bag and leave to strain for a few hours or overnight, but not more than 24 hours.

3 Measure the strained juice. For each 600 ml (1 pint) juice, weigh 450 g (1 lb) sugar. Pour the juice into a clean preserving pan. Warm the sugar (see box, page 44), and add it to the juice. Stir over a low heat until the sugar has completely dissolved.

4 Increase the heat and boil the mixture rapidly, without stirring, for 9–10 minutes, or until it reaches setting point. Test for set and skim off any scum (see box, page 46). Stir in the port.

5 Immediately pour the jelly into warmed sterilized jars, tilting them slightly to prevent air pockets from forming. Seal the jars and label.

Makes about 1.4 kg (3 lb)

MINT AND APPLE JELLY

INGREDIENTS

1.4 kg (3 lb) cooking apples

600 ml (1 pint) water

300 ml (10 fl oz) cider vinegar

225 g (8 oz) fresh mint

sugar

2–3 drops of green food colouring (optional)

Jelly-making equipment

1 Chop the apples without peeling or coring them. Put them into a preserving pan with the water and vinegar. Strip the mint leaves from their stalks and set aside. Add the stalks to the pan. Bring the mixture to a boil, and simmer for about 40 minutes, or until the apples are very soft and pulpy.

2 While the apples are cooking, prepare the jelly bag for straining the fruit. Scald it by evenly pouring through boiling water, squeeze it well, then use as directed (see box, above). Pour the fruit pulp into the jelly bag and leave to strain for a few hours or overnight, but not more than 24 hours.

3 Measure the strained juice. For each 600 ml (1 pint) juice, weigh 450 g (1 lb) sugar. Pour the juice into a clean preserving pan. Warm the sugar (see box, page 44), and add it to the juice. Stir over a low heat until the sugar has completely dissolved. Tie half of the mint leaves in a muslin bag and add to the jelly mixture. Increase the heat and boil the mixture rapidly, without stirring, for 15 minutes, or until it reaches setting point. Test for set and skim off any scum (see box, page 46).

4 Remove the muslin bag, squeezing any juice back into the pan; discard the bag. Chop the remaining mint leaves. Stir in the freshly chopped mint and green food colouring, if using.

5 Immediately pour the jelly into warmed sterilized jars, tilting them slightly to prevent air pockets from forming. Seal the jars and label.

Makes about 675 g (1½ lb)

VARIATIONS
Other herb and apple jellies can be made using the same method as for mint. Parsley, thyme, rosemary, and sage are all equally good.

CRANBERRY AND APPLE JELLY

Ruby-red cranberries are popular for festive occasions in the United States. In this recipe they are teamed up with apples, creating a tart, garnet-coloured jelly. Cranberry and Apple Jelly is a delicious accompaniment to roast pork, cold meats, and poultry – especially roast turkey.

INGREDIENTS

1.4 kg (3 lb) cooking apples

1 kg (2 lb) fresh cranberries

1.15 litres (2 pints) water

about 1 kg (2 lb) sugar

Makes about 1.6 kg (3¹/₂ lb)

1 ◄ Cut out any bruised or damaged parts from the apples, then coarsely chop the apples without peeling or coring them.

2 ▼ Put the apples into a preserving pan with the fresh cranberries.

3 ▲ Pour in the water just to cover the fruits, adding a little more if necessary, and bring to a boil. Simmer for 30 minutes, or until the fruits are very soft and pulpy.

4 While the apples and cranberries are cooking, prepare a jelly bag for straining the fruits. Scald the jelly bag by evenly pouring through boiling water, squeeze it well, then suspend over a large non-metallic bowl.

5 ▶ Ladle the fruit pulp into the jelly bag and leave to strain for a few hours, or overnight, but not more than 24 hours. Make sure that the jelly bag is not squeezed or shaken while the pulp is straining, or the jelly will be cloudy.

6 ▲ Measure the strained juice. For each 600 ml (1 pint) juice, weigh 450 g (1 lb) sugar. Pour the juice into a clean preserving pan. Warm the sugar (see box, page 46), and add it to the juice. Stir over a low heat, with a wooden spoon, until the sugar has completely dissolved.

7 ▲ Increase the heat and boil the mixture rapidly, without stirring, for 10–12 minutes, or until it reaches setting point. Remove the pan from the heat to test for set and skim off any scum (see box, page 46). Immediately pour the jelly into warmed sterilized jars, tilting them slightly to prevent air pockets from forming. Seal the jars and label.

Apple and Orange Jelly

INGREDIENTS

1.15 kg (2¹/₂ lb) cooking apples

3 oranges

1.15 litres (2 pints) water

sugar

WARMING SUGAR In these jelly recipes the amount of sugar required is calculated according to the amount of strained juice you have after the fruit is cooked. It is therefore difficult to be specific with an exact amount of sugar in the ingredients list, so make sure you have a good supply before you start. After weighing the sugar, it can be warmed so it dissolves quicker in the juice. Put the oven on its lowest setting, and put the sugar into an ovenproof bowl. Warm the sugar for about 15 minutes.

1 Peel, core, and chop the apples, reserving the cores and pips. Chop the unpeeled oranges and remove the pips. Put the apple cores and apple and orange pips on a square of muslin and tie up tightly into a bag with a long piece of string.

2 Put the chopped fruits with the water into a preserving pan and bring to a boil. Simmer for 50 minutes, or until the fruits are soft and pulpy. Remove and discard the muslin bag.

3 While the apples and oranges are cooking, prepare the jelly bag for straining the fruits. Scald it by evenly pouring through boiling water, squeeze it well, then use as directed (see box, page 41). Pour the fruit pulp into the jelly bag and leave to strain for a few hours or overnight, but not more than 24 hours.

4 Measure the strained juice. For each 600 ml (1 pint) juice, weigh 450 g (1 lb) sugar. Pour the juice into a clean preserving pan. Warm the sugar (see box, left), and add it to the juice. Stir over a low heat until the sugar has completely dissolved.

5 Increase the heat and boil the mixture rapidly, without stirring, for 10–12 minutes, or until it reaches setting point. Test for set and skim off any scum (see box, page 46).

6 Pour the jelly into warmed sterilized jars, tilting them slightly to prevent air pockets from forming. Seal the jars and label.

Makes about 1.6 kg (3¹/₂ lb)

Mixed Fruit Jelly

INGREDIENTS

450 g (1 lb) cooking apples

4 large oranges

1 lemon

1.75 litres (3 pints) water

450 g (1 lb) strawberries

sugar

1 Coarsely chop the apples, oranges, and lemon, without peeling, pipping, or coring them. Put them into a preserving pan with the water. Bring to a boil, and simmer for 40–45 minutes, or until the fruits are very soft and pulpy.

2 Hull and halve the strawberries and add them to the pan. Bring the mixture back to a boil, and simmer for 5 minutes, or until the strawberries are very soft.

3 While the strawberries are cooking, prepare the jelly bag for straining the fruits. Scald it by evenly pouring through boiling water, squeeze it well, then use as directed (see box, page 41). Pour the fruit pulp into the jelly bag and leave to strain for a few hours or overnight, but not more than 24 hours.

4 Measure the strained juice. For each 600 ml (1 pint) juice, weigh 450 g (1 lb) sugar. Pour the juice into a clean preserving pan. Warm the sugar (see box, above), and add it to the juice. Stir over a low heat until the sugar has completely dissolved.

5 Increase the heat and boil the mixture rapidly, without stirring, for 30–35 minutes, or until it reaches setting point. Test for set and skim off any scum (see box, page 46). Immediately pour the jelly into warmed sterilized jars, tilting them slightly to prevent air pockets from forming. Seal the jars and label.

Makes about 1.5 kg (3¹/₄ lb)

CHILLI AND APPLE JELLY

INGREDIENTS

1.4 kg (3 lb) cooking apples

600 ml (1 pint) water

300 ml (10 fl oz) cider vinegar

100 g (4 oz) fresh green chillies

sugar

2–3 drops of green food colouring (optional)

1 Chop the apples without peeling or coring them. Put them into a preserving pan with the water and vinegar.

2 Trim the chillies and cut in half lengthways. Remove and discard the seeds. Add the chillies to the pan with the apples.

3 Bring the mixture to a boil, and simmer for 20–25 minutes, or until the fruit is very soft and pulpy.

4 While the apples and chillies are cooking, prepare the jelly bag for straining the fruits. Scald it by evenly pouring through boiling water, squeeze it well, then use as directed (see box, page 41). Pour the pulp into the jelly bag and leave to strain for a few hours or overnight, but not more than 24 hours.

5 Measure the strained juice. For each 600 ml (1 pint) juice, weigh 450 g (1 lb) sugar. Pour the juice into a clean preserving pan. Warm the sugar (see box, page 44) and add it to the juice. Stir over a low heat until the sugar has completely dissolved.

6 Increase the heat and boil the mixture rapidly, without stirring, for 8–10 minutes, or until it reaches setting point. Test for set and skim off any scum (see box, page 46).

7 Stir in the food colouring, if using. Immediately pour the jelly into warmed sterilized jars, tilting them slightly to prevent air pockets from forming. Seal the jars and label.

Makes about 450 g (1 lb)

COOK'S TIP
Chillies should be prepared with care. Wear rubber gloves when handling them, as it can be painful if any chilli gets on the skin, eyes, or nose. Afterwards, wash all surfaces and equipment which have come into contact with the chillies.

GRAPE JELLY

INGREDIENTS

1.4 kg (3 lb) green grapes

juice of 2 lemons

600 ml (1 pint) water

sugar

*CHAMELEON
Despite using green grapes, Grape Jelly has a pink hue.*

1 Coarsely chop the grapes. Put them into a preserving pan with the lemon juice and water. Bring the mixture to a boil, and simmer for 30 minutes, or until the fruit is very soft and pulpy.

2 While the grapes are cooking, prepare the jelly bag for straining the fruits. Scald it by evenly pouring through boiling water, squeeze it well, then use as directed (see box, page 41). Pour the fruit pulp into the jelly bag and leave to strain for a few hours or overnight, but not more than 24 hours.

3 Measure the strained juice. For each 600 ml (1 pint) juice, weigh 450 g (1 lb) sugar. Pour the juice into a clean preserving pan. Warm the sugar (see box, page 44), and add it to the juice. Stir over a low heat until the sugar has completely dissolved.

4 Increase the heat and boil the mixture rapidly, without stirring, for 12 minutes, or until it reaches setting point. Test for set and skim off any scum (see box, page 46).

5 Immediately pour the jelly into warmed sterilized jars, tilting them slightly to prevent air pockets from forming. Seal the jars and label.

Makes about 675 g (1¹/2 lb)

BRAMBLE JELLY

INGREDIENTS

2.25 kg (5 lb) blackberries

juice of 2 lemons

900 ml (1½ pints) water

sugar

1 Put the blackberries into a preserving pan with the lemon juice and water. Bring to a boil, and simmer for 30 minutes, or until the fruit is very soft and pulpy.

2 While the blackberries are cooking, prepare the jelly bag for straining the fruit. Scald it by evenly pouring through boiling water, squeeze it well, then use as directed (see box, page 41). Pour the fruit pulp into the jelly bag and leave the blackberry pulp to strain for a few hours or overnight, but not more than 24 hours.

3 Measure the strained juice. For each 600 ml (1 pint) juice, weigh 450 g (1 lb) sugar. Pour the juice into a clean preserving pan. Warm the sugar (see box, page 44), and add it to the juice. Stir over a low heat, with a wooden spoon, until the sugar has completely dissolved.

4 Increase the heat and boil the mixture rapidly, without stirring, for 9–10 minutes, or until it reaches setting point. Test for set and skim off any scum (see box, left).

5 Immediately pour the jelly into warmed sterilized jars, tilting them slightly to prevent air pockets from forming. Seal the jars and label.

Makes about 1.4 kg (3 lb)

TESTING FOR SET AND SKIMMING JELLIES

Remove the pan from the heat. The best way to test for set is with a sugar thermometer, which should read 104°C (220°F) when setting point is reached. If you do not have a thermometer, use the cold plate test: drop a little of the jelly on a cold plate and chill quickly in the refrigerator. If it forms a skin and wrinkles when pushed with a finger, it should be ready. Lightly skim off any scum from the surface of the jelly, using a long-handled metal spoon.

CRAB APPLE JELLY

INGREDIENTS

2.75 kg (6 lb) crab apples

juice of 2 lemons

1.75 litres (3 pints) water

5 whole cloves

sugar

1 Coarsely chop the crab apples without peeling or coring them. Put them into a preserving pan with the lemon juice, water, and cloves. Bring the mixture to a boil, and simmer for 40 minutes, or until the fruit is very soft and pulpy.

2 While the apples are cooking, prepare the jelly bag for straining the fruit. Scald it by evenly pouring through boiling water, squeeze it well, then use as directed (see box, page 41). Pour the fruit pulp into the jelly bag and leave to strain for a few hours or overnight, but not more than 24 hours.

3 Measure the strained juice. For each 600 ml (1 pint) juice, weigh 450 g (1 lb) sugar. Pour the juice into a clean preserving pan. Warm the sugar (see box, page 44), and add it to the juice. Stir over a low heat until the sugar has completely dissolved.

4 Increase the heat and boil the mixture rapidly, without stirring, for 9–10 minutes, or until it reaches setting point. Test for set and skim off any scum (see box, above).

5 Immediately pour the jelly into warmed sterilized jars, tilting them slightly to prevent air pockets from forming. Seal the jars and label.

Makes about 1.8 kg (4 lb)

FRUIT BUTTERS & CHEESES

A GLUT OF sun-ripened fruits, available in the shops at bargain prices, means it is the time to make fruit butters and cheeses. They are so easy to prepare and require no special skill or equipment except a good wooden spoon for stirring. The bitter-sweet flavour and smooth spreadable texture of butters make them an ideal substitute for ordinary butter on bread, toast, scones, and cake. Fruit cheeses are more substantial, and they look good when set in shapely moulds, then turned out and sliced, cubed, or cut into wedges, whether sprinkled with sugar or not.

Although they have a very long history stretching back over thousands of years, fruit cheeses have never gone out of fashion or lost their popularity around the world. In the south of France, they are served together with fresh cheeses; in Mexico and Brazil, guavas, quinces, mangoes, and pineapples are all used for making fruit cheeses, which are eaten with cream cheese and crackers. Closer to home, orchard fruits, such as plums and damsons, make very colourful butters and cheeses.

MAKING FRUIT BUTTERS & CHEESES

❧ Choose the ingredients. Most fruits can be used, but sharply flavoured ones, such as blackberries, plums, quinces, and damsons work best. Spices can be added. Granulated sugar is the recommended sweetener.

❧ Wash, stone or hull, and chop the fruits as necessary, removing any mouldy or damaged parts. Put the fruits into a preserving pan. (Lightly greasing the pan first helps prevent the fruits from sticking.) Barely cover the fruits with water and bring to a boil, then simmer, stirring occasionally over a low heat, until the fruits are soft and pulpy and there is no excess liquid. Sieve or liquidize the fruits to a purée.

❧ Weigh the pulp. For butters, weigh 225–350 g (8–12 oz) sugar for each 450 g (1 lb) pulp. For cheeses, weigh 450 g (1 lb) sugar for each 450 g (1 lb) pulp. Warm the sugar (see box, page 44). Return the pulp to the pan with the sugar, add spices if using, and stir over a low heat until the sugar has completely dissolved.

❧ Bring to a boil and simmer, 30–45 minutes for butters, and 45–60 minutes for cheeses, stirring frequently to prevent them from burning. The butter is ready when a spoonful placed on a saucer does not exude any liquid.

The cheese is ready when a spoon drawn across the bottom of the pan leaves a clean line.

❧ Spoon butters into sterilized jars (see page 11), and seal. For cheeses, pour the mixture into moulds, from which they can be turned out for slicing. Brush the moulds with a little glycerine, so they will slip out easily.

How to seal and store
Screw-top lids are the best choice for sealing fruit butters, because butters have a tendency to dry out, and need an airtight seal. Butters, which have a thick spreading consistency, do not keep quite as well as jams and should be used up within 3 months. If cheeses are in moulds, cover them as you would jams, with wax discs and cellophane circles (see page 15). Cheeses have a higher sugar content than butters and will keep for up to 1 year.

What can go wrong and why
If the butter starts to ferment, this could be a result either of too short a cooking time or of too little sugar. The mixtures may caramelize if the excess water has not evaporated before adding the sugar.

STRAWBERRY-PEAR BUTTER

The flavours of summer and autumn blend together in this thick, creamy butter. Serve it in summer spooned on to freshly made pancakes with sliced strawberries and cream, or on a winter's afternoon spread on hot buttered scones or toast. Small jars of this fruit butter also make pretty gifts for special occasions.

INGREDIENTS

1.8 kg (4 lb) pears

450 g (1 lb) strawberries

300 ml (10 fl oz) water

2.5 ml (¹/₂ tsp) ground cinnamon

sugar

Makes about 775 g (1³/4 lb)

1 ▼ Peel the pears, cut into quarters, and remove and discard the cores. Chop the pears finely. Hull the strawberries and cut them into quarters.

2 Put the pears and strawberries into a preserving pan. Add the water and ground cinnamon and bring to a boil. Simmer, stirring occasionally, for 1–1¹/₄ hours, or until the fruits are soft. The mixture should be thick and pulpy, and all of the excess liquid should have evaporated.

3 ◄ With the back of a wooden spoon, press the fruit mixture through a plastic sieve set over a non-metallic bowl. Weigh the sieved pulp. For each 450 g (1 lb) pulp, weigh 350 g (12 oz) sugar. Warm the sugar (see box, page 44).

4 Stir the mixture over a low heat, with a wooden spoon, until the sugar has completely dissolved.

5 ▼ Return the pulp to the pan, add the sugar, and simmer over a low heat, stirring frequently, until the butter thickens to resemble clotted cream. This will take 15–20 minutes. The butter is ready when a spoonful placed on a saucer does not exude any liquid.

6 Remove the pan from the heat. Spoon the butter into warmed sterilized jars, to within 3 mm (¹/₈ inch) of the tops. Seal the jars and label.

PEACH BUTTER

INGREDIENTS

1 kg (2 lb) ripe peaches

480 ml (16 fl oz) water

sugar

1 Drop the peaches into boiling water for 1–2 minutes, then transfer to a bowl of iced water. Drain the peaches when cool.

2 Halve the peaches, peel, and coarsely chop the flesh. Put the flesh into a saucepan with the measured water. Simmer, stirring occasionally, for 20 minutes, or until very soft. Press the mixture through a plastic sieve set over a non-metallic bowl.

3 Weigh the sieved pulp. For each 225 g (8 oz) pulp, weigh 100 g (4 oz) sugar. Warm the sugar (see box, page 44). Return the pulp to the pan, add the sugar, and stir over a low heat until the sugar has completely dissolved. Simmer over a low heat, stirring frequently, for 30 minutes, or until the butter thickens to resemble clotted cream.

4 Spoon the butter into warmed sterilized jars, seal, and label.

Makes about 450 g (1 lb)

CRANBERRY BUTTER

INGREDIENTS

1.4 kg (3 lb) fresh cranberries

300 ml (10 fl oz) water

sugar

1 Put the cranberries into a saucepan with the water and bring to a boil. Simmer, stirring occasionally, for 35–40 minutes, or until the cranberries are very soft. Press the mixture through a plastic sieve set over a non-metallic bowl.

2 Weigh the sieved pulp. For each 450 g (1 lb) pulp, weigh 350 g (12 oz) sugar. Warm the sugar (see box, page 44). Return the pulp to the pan, add the sugar, and stir over a low heat until the sugar has completely dissolved.

3 Simmer over a low heat, stirring frequently, for 1 hour, or until the butter thickens to resemble clotted cream.

4 Spoon the butter into warmed sterilized jars, seal, and label.

Makes about 1.15 kg (2¹/₂ lb)

CIDER-APPLE BUTTER

INGREDIENTS

1 kg (2 lb) eating apples

1 kg (2 lb) cooking apples

240 ml (8 fl oz) cider

sugar

5 ml (1 tsp) ground coriander

1 Coarsely chop the apples, without peeling or coring them. Put the apples into a saucepan, add the cider, and bring to a boil. Simmer, stirring occasionally, for 25–30 minutes, or until the apples are very soft. Press the mixture through a plastic sieve set over a non-metallic bowl.

2 Weigh the sieved pulp. For each 100 g (4 oz) pulp, weigh 50 g (2 oz) sugar. Warm the sugar (see box, page 44). Return the pulp to the pan, add the sugar and coriander, and stir over a low heat until the sugar has completely dissolved.

3 Simmer over a low heat, stirring frequently, for 30 minutes, or until the butter thickens to resemble clotted cream.

4 Spoon the butter into warmed sterilized jars, seal, and label.

Makes about 675 g (1¹/₂ lb)

VARIATION
Give a slightly tangier taste to this all-time favourite butter by using Spiced Pickling Vinegar (see recipe, page 120) in place of the cider, and ground cinnamon instead of the coriander. Add the finely grated zest of 1 lemon with the spice.

DAMSON CHEESE

INGREDIENTS

2.75 kg (6 lb) damsons

300 ml (10 fl oz) water

sugar, warmed
(see box, page 44)

1 Put the damsons and water into a preserving pan and bring to a boil. Simmer, stirring occasionally, for 30 minutes, or until tender.

2 Press the damsons and juice through a plastic sieve set over a non-metallic bowl. Discard the stones. Weigh the sieved pulp and return it to the pan with an equal weight of warmed sugar. Stir over a low heat until the sugar has completely dissolved.

3 Bring to a boil and simmer, stirring frequently, for 40–45 minutes. The pulp should be thick and firm enough that when a wooden spoon is drawn across the bottom of the pan, it will not move.

4 Spoon the cheese into warmed sterilized jars, to within 3 mm (1/8 inch) of the tops. Seal and label.

Makes about 1.8 kg (4 lb)

GUAVA CHEESE

INGREDIENTS

450 g (1 lb) canned guavas

225 g (8 oz) sugar, warmed
(see box, page 44)

30 ml (2 tbsp) lemon juice

This cheese is a quick, no-fuss preserve with lots of tropical flavour.

1 Strain the guavas and measure the juice. You will need 100 ml (4 fl oz) guava juice from the can. Chop the guavas coarsely and put with the measured juice into a food processor. Purée the mixture until it is smooth.

2 Put the purée, warmed sugar, and lemon juice into a saucepan. Stir over a low heat until the sugar has completely dissolved. Simmer over a low heat for 12 minutes. The pulp should be thick and firm enough that when a wooden spoon is drawn across the bottom of the pan, it will not move.

3 Spoon the cheese into warmed sterilized jars, to within 3 mm (1/8 inch) of the tops. Seal and label.

Makes about 350 g (12 oz)

DID YOU KNOW?
Guavas are an oval tropical fruit with a yellow to green skin and an off-white to red flesh. Fresh guavas are difficult to obtain, so this easy recipe is made with canned guavas.

PLUM AND LEMON CHEESE

INGREDIENTS

2.75 kg (6 lb) plums

300 ml (10 fl oz) water

sugar, warmed
(see box, page 44)

finely grated zest and juice
of 2 lemons

1 Put the plums and water into a preserving pan and bring to a boil. Simmer, stirring occasionally, for 30 minutes.

2 Press the plums and juice through a plastic sieve set over a non-metallic bowl. Discard the stones. Weigh the sieved pulp and return it to the pan with an equal weight of warmed sugar. Add the lemon zest and juice. Stir over a low heat until the sugar has completely dissolved.

3 Bring to a boil, then simmer over a low heat, stirring frequently, for 40–45 minutes. The pulp should be thick and firm enough that when a wooden spoon is drawn across the bottom of the pan, it will not move.

4 Spoon the cheese into warmed sterilized jars, to within 3 mm (1/8 inch) of the tops. Seal and label.

Makes about 1.8 kg (4 lb)

FRUIT CURDS

LEMON CURD TARTS, with their sharp, fruity flavour, are what we think of when curds are mentioned today, unless of course our minds stray back to childhood and Little Miss Muffet, who ate curds and whey until she was disturbed by a spider. These curd recipes, unlike Miss Muffet's curds, are enriched with butter and eggs. Although lemon curd is an undoubted favourite, there are other, equally delicate and delicious, fruit curds to beguile our palates and to take as gifts to friends. Oranges, limes, and other fruits can be used, and there is plenty of room for experimentation.

Curds have the paradoxical virtue of not being good keepers. They must be refrigerated, and should not be left to languish on the refrigerator shelf, but used within a month. In any case, these preserves are better eaten sooner than later because their flavour does fade and their fresh quality is lost the longer they are kept.

Curds can be spread on bread, toast, or on plain cake. They can also form the base of a dessert, or be spooned over ice-cream with colourful pieces of fruit. And what better way to spend a miserably wet Sunday afternoon in winter than making a batch of curd tarts, baked in shortcrust pastry that melts in the mouth, which recreate teatimes of the past?

MAKING FRUIT CURDS

❧ Select fresh ingredients, particularly fresh eggs. Caster sugar is the preferred sweetener, because curds are cooked very gently and the fine granules will dissolve more easily.
❧ Finely grate the zest of the chosen citrus fruits and squeeze out the juice. Strain and measure the juice. Pour it into a non-metallic bowl set over a pan of gently simmering water (or use a double boiler), and add the grated zest, butter, and sugar. Stir the mixture over a low heat, with a wooden spoon, until the butter has melted and the sugar has completely dissolved. Lightly beat the eggs and strain into the mixture. Continue simmering, stirring, until the mixture has thickened enough to coat the back of the spoon. Do not allow the contents of the bowl to boil. Curds require long slow cooking, so do not rush the process by increasing the heat.
❧ When the mixture has thickened, immediately pour it into warmed sterilized jars (see page 11). Because of their limited shelf life, curds are best made in small quantities and put into 225 g (8 oz) jars. Fill them right to the tops, because the curd will shrink and thicken as it cools.

How to seal and store
Use wax discs and cellophane circles, because they help prevent curds from going mouldy. Place a wax disc, wax-side down, on the top of the curd, smooth over to remove any air pockets, and leave to cool. Put a dampened cellophane circle over the top, and secure with an elastic band. Label and keep in the refrigerator. Use within 1 month.

What can go wrong and why
If a curd is runny, it has been insufficiently cooked. If it is curdled, it was cooked over too high a heat.

LIGHTLY COOKED EGGS Curds are cooked over a gentle heat and do not reach a high enough temperature to thoroughly cook the eggs. If you are worried about the slight risk of salmonella from lightly cooked eggs, it is best not to eat curds.

LEMON CURD

The tang of this spread comes from the lively lemon, and the thick, luscious smoothness from the careful blending of fresh eggs, creamy butter, and fine-grained sugar. Lemon curd will only keep for a month in the refrigerator, but it is so delicious that it is unlikely to last this long anyway. Serve it on toast, in tarts, or as a filling for cakes.

INGREDIENTS

6–8 large juicy lemons

225 g (8 oz) unsalted butter

575 g (1 lb 4 oz) caster sugar

5 eggs (size 1)

Makes about 1.15 kg (2 1/2 lb)

WAXED LEMONS
If the lemons are waxed, scrub them to remove the coating before grating the zest.

1 ▶ Grate the zest from the lemons on the finest side of the grater. Squeeze the juice and strain it into a large measuring jug. You will need 300 ml (10 fl oz) juice.

2 ▼ Cut the butter into small pieces. Put the pieces of butter into a glass bowl, along with the sugar, lemon zest and juice, set over a pan of gently simmering water. The bottom of the bowl should not touch the water, nor should the water boil rapidly. Stir the mixture until the butter has melted and the sugar has completely dissolved.

3 ▼ Lightly beat the eggs in a bowl, but do not whisk them. Strain the eggs through a plastic sieve into the lemon mixture. Simmer over a low heat, stirring constantly with a wooden spoon, until the mixture thickens slightly. This will take 20–25 minutes. Do not allow the mixture to boil or it will curdle.

4 ▲ As soon as the mixture is thick enough to coat the back of the spoon, remove the bowl from the pan of water.

5 ▲ Pour into warmed sterilized jars. Place a wax disc, wax-side down, on top of each jar. Smooth over to remove any air pockets. Leave to cool.

6 ▲ Cover with dampened cellophane circles. Label, and store the curd in the refrigerator.

MORE CURD FLAVOURS

Oranges, limes, and grapefruit all make delicious curds. By adapting the Lemon Curd recipe you can create a sweeter or tangier preserve. For a touch of sophistication, add a splash or two of a flavoured liqueur.

Orange Curd
This curd is delicious served with warm pancakes and whipped cream, particularly if you squeeze extra orange juice on top. Follow the recipe for Lemon Curd, using the juice of 3 medium oranges and the juice of 1 lemon instead of the juice of 6–8 lemons. Combine the squeezed juices from the oranges and lemon to obtain a total of 300 ml (10 fl oz).

Above, Lime Curd; right, Orange Curd

Lime Curd
Use limes to make a tangier spread; the juice and tiny flecks of grated zest will turn the curd a subtle shade of green. Lime Curd makes an unusual filling for a sponge cake, or a tasty topping for ice cream. You will need more limes than lemons for this curd, about 10 juicy ones, to get the 300 ml (10 fl oz) juice required.

Pink Grapefruit and Lime Curd
◄ Use the finely grated zest of 2 pink grapefruit and 1 lime for this curd, and combine the juices to ensure you have the amount you need. If the curd is too runny, thicken it by sprinkling a little ground rice into the mixture, stirring it in well.

Tipsy Curd
Stir a few spoonfuls of a rich liqueur, such as advocaat, into the finished curd. Tipsy curd is delicious when spread generously in a pastry pie shell, then piled high with sliced tropical fruits.

DID YOU KNOW?
Tangy fruit curds, simply spread on bread or between layers of sponge cake, were popular teatime treats in Victorian and Edwardian England. They were also used as a fragrant filling for trifles, and piped into tartlets in elegant sweet swirls.
In her book *Modern Cookery for Private Families,* the nineteenth-century cookery writer Eliza Acton used a type of lemon curd as a filling for little puff pastry tarts. In addition to eggs, sugar, pounded butter, and lemon, she instructed the reader to "strew lightly in a spoonful of flour, well dried and sifted". Most modern fruit curds do not include flour, although the idea of adding a thickener is a good one if the curd seems a little on the runny side – ground rice is suggested in Pink Grapefruit and Lime Curd for this reason.

FRUITS IN ALCOHOL
& FLAVOURED DRINKS

FRUITS IN ALCOHOL

NOTHING IS quite so luxurious as fruit that has soaked up the perfumes of fortified wine, spirits, or liqueurs and, in turn, given its own flavour to the macerating liquid. Something quite astonishing happens to everyday pitted prunes when they have spent some time immersed in port.

Rum, gin, and brandy all have a strong affinity for summer and autumn fruits, but almost any kind of alcohol can be used. Kirsch, for example, complements full-flavoured fruits, such as raspberries, blackberries, loganberries, and pineapples, whisky steeps well with grapes, and apricots take on a wonderful new flavour after being soaked in orange curaçao. Some cooked fruits can be preserved in wine, but they will last longer if used in combination with a spirit.

Fruits in alcohol, sweetened with sugar, look beautiful, taste even better, and are easy to make with only a little time and effort. They are superb when served as desserts, especially when topped with whipped cream, and their richness makes them great accompaniments to roast meats, game, and poultry, especially duck.

MAKING FRUITS IN ALCOHOL

❧ Choose your fruits; they must be just ripe. If they are over-ripe they will not retain their shape in the alcohol. Pick over the fruits, removing any mouldy or damaged parts. Wash and dry the fruits and remove stones, if necessary. Remove and discard any excess peel, pips, and cores from fruits such as pears. Soft fruits, such as berries, blackcurrants, apricots, and peaches, can be used raw, while firmer ones, such as apples and hard plums, may require light cooking first.

❧ Pack the fruits into sterilized jars (see page 11), either in layers with sugar or in a sugar syrup. Warm the jars if the ingredients used are hot. White granulated sugar is the usual choice of sweetener, but light brown sugar can be used for flavour, or if a darker colour is preferred. Shake the jars once or twice during the early days of storage, to help dissolve the sugar (unless a syrup is used) and blend it with the alcohol.

❧ Pour the chosen alcohol over the fruits to completely cover them, making sure that there are no air pockets between them. The amount of liquid can vary, depending on the size of the fruits and the amount of sugar used, so make sure you have plenty of the chosen alcohol in stock.

❧ Spices, such as whole cloves, cinnamon sticks, and allspice berries can be added to the fruits for extra flavour.

How to seal and store

Seal tightly, preferably with non-corrosive, screw-top lids. An airtight seal is required to prevent the alcohol from evaporating. Leave the fruits in a cool dark place for at least 1 month, and preferably longer, before using, to allow the flavours to develop. Shake the jars from time to time to blend the sugar and flavourings. As long as the fruits are covered by the alcohol, they should keep for about 1 year, and the flavour will improve over this time.

What can go wrong and why

Some fruits have a tendency to float to the top of the liquid. Prevent this either by filling the jar with fruits to the very top, or by placing a piece of crumpled greaseproof paper in the top of the jar to hold the fruits down. Remove the paper after about 1 week, after which time the fruits should remain in place. Make sure the fruits are covered with alcohol before re-sealing the jar. If the alcohol has evaporated, and left the fruits exposed, the jar has not been sealed tightly enough.

SUMMER FRUITS IN KIRSCH

A delicious way to preserve soft fruits, this recipe can be made either all at once, or throughout the summer as the different fruits ripen. If you layer the fruit over a period of time, keep it below the level of the alcohol by putting a lightly weighted coffee saucer or some crumpled greaseproof paper in the jar. When the last fruits have been added, top up with kirsch, and re-seal.

INGREDIENTS

675 g (1¹/₂ lb) mixed summer fruits, e.g. raspberries, boysenberries, blueberries, small strawberries, blackberries, redcurrants, whitecurrants, and blackcurrants

250 g (9 oz) sugar

about 300 ml (10 fl oz) kirsch

Fills one 1 litre (1 ³/₄ pint) jar

1 ◄Pick over the fruits, removing any leaves, mouldy or damaged parts, hulls, and stalks. For the currants, run a fork along the stalks to remove the berries. Wash the fruits in a plastic sieve or colander and dry on kitchen paper.

2 ▶ Layer the fruits and sugar in a sterilized jar to within 2.5 cm (1 inch) of the top of the jar.

TWICE THE FUN
Alcohol-drenched fruits make an intoxicating dessert, while the berry-flavoured kirsch can be drunk separately.

3 ▲Pour in the kirsch to cover the fruits by about 1.25 cm (¹/₂ inch), making sure there are no air pockets left between the fruits. Seal the jar and label.

4 Keep in a cool dark place for 2–3 months before using, to allow the flavours to develop, tipping the jar occasionally so the sugar dissolves.

Mangoes in Brandy

INGREDIENTS

3–4 large mangoes

225 g (8 oz) sugar

450 ml (15 fl oz) brandy

1 Cut each mango on both sides of the stone, slice the flesh away from the stone, and discard the stone. Peel the mango slices and cut the flesh into even-sized chunks. There should be about 1 kg (2 lb) mango chunks.

2 Pack the mango cubes into sterilized jars, layering them with the sugar as you go. Leave 2.5 cm (1 inch) at the tops of the jars.

3 Pour in the brandy to cover the mango by 1.25 cm ($^1/_2$ inch), making sure there are no air pockets between the fruits. Seal the jars, label, and shake well.

4 Keep in a cool dark place for at least 2 months before using, to allow the flavours to develop. Shake from time to time during the first week of storage, to make sure all the sugar dissolves in the brandy.

Fills about three 480 ml (16 fl oz) jars

Pears in Vodka

INGREDIENTS

1 kg (2 lb) ripe pears

450 g (1 lb) sugar

600–750 ml (1–1$^1/_4$ pints) vodka

1 Peel, quarter, and core the pears quickly to prevent discoloration. Pack the pears into sterilized jars, layering them with the sugar as you go. Leave 2.5 cm (1 inch) at the tops of the jars.

2 Pour in the vodka to cover the pears by 1.25 cm ($^1/_2$ inch), making sure there are no air pockets between the fruits. Seal the jars, label, and shake well.

3 Keep in a cool dark place for at least 2–3 months before using, to allow the flavours to develop. Shake from time to time during the first week of storage, to make sure all the sugar dissolves.

Fills about two 750 ml (1$^1/_4$ pint) jars

Plums in Rum

INGREDIENTS

1.4 kg (3 lb) plums

225 g (8 oz) sugar

100 ml (4 fl oz) water

350 ml (12 fl oz) golden rum

RUMTOPF Use a mixture of fruits, such as cherries, strawberries, apricots, nectarines, and plums, to make a traditional *Rumtopf*. This German preserve is made in stages as the fruits become available, to keep until Advent. Layer each addition of fruit with sugar and cover with rum as directed.

1 Prick the plums all over with a sterilized needle or a wooden cocktail stick. In a saucepan, combine the sugar and water and simmer over a low heat, stirring with a wooden spoon, until the sugar has completely dissolved. Add the plums and simmer for 5 minutes. Remove the pan from the heat and allow to cool.

2 Pack the plums and syrup into sterilized jars, then pour in the rum to cover them by 2.5 cm (1 inch). Seal the jars and label.

3 Keep in a cool dark place for at least 1 month before using, to allow the flavours to develop. Check after the first day or so that the plums are still covered by the liquid; add more rum, if necessary and re-seal.

Fills about four 600 ml (1 pint) jars

PRUNES IN PORT

INGREDIENTS

500 g (1 lb 2 oz) stoned
prunes

480–600 ml (16–20 fl oz)
tawny port

Serve the prunes with roast pork or game, or as a simple dessert with ice cream, spooning the port over it. Or drink the port as a liqueur.

1 Pack the prunes into a sterilized jar and pour in about 480 ml (16 fl oz) port to cover the prunes by 4 cm (1½ inches). Cover and reserve the remaining port.

2 Seal the jar and label. Keep the prunes in a cool dark place.

3 Check the prunes in a day or two. Once they have soaked up so much port that they are no longer covered, pour in the remaining port. Re-seal and leave for 1 month before using, to allow the flavours to develop.

Fills one 1 litre (1¾ pint) jar

TIPSY APRICOTS

INGREDIENTS

675 g–1 kg (1½–2 lb)
apricots, according to size

350 g (12 oz) sugar

240–300 ml (8–10 fl oz)
orange curaçao

240–300 ml (8–10 fl oz) dark
rum

1 Prick the apricots all over with a sterilized needle or a wooden cocktail stick.

2 Pack the apricots into sterilized jars, layering them with the sugar as you go. Leave 2.5 cm (1 inch) at the tops of the jars.

3 Mix the orange curaçao with the rum in a glass measuring jug. Pour the mixed alcohols into the jars to cover the apricots by 1.25 cm (½ inch), making sure there are no air pockets between the fruits.

4 Seal the jars and label. Shake the jars well so that the sugar can start to blend and dissolve into the alcohol.

5 Keep in a cool dark place for at least 2 months before using, to allow the flavours to develop. Shake from time to time during the first week to of storage, to make sure all the sugar dissolves in the alcohol.

Fills about two 750 ml (1¼ pint) jars

VARIATION
Mandarins or clementines can be preserved in the same syrup as apricots. Peel the fruits, keeping them whole (there is no need to prick them). Pack into jars, layering with the sugar, add the grated zest of 2 oranges, and continue as directed in step 3.

PEARS IN BRANDY

INGREDIENTS

1.4 kg (3 lb) firm ripe pears

100 g (4 oz) sugar

480 ml (16 fl oz) brandy

1 Peel, quarter, and core the pears. If the fruits are small, just halve and core them.

2 Put the pear quarters and the sugar into a saucepan with just enough water to cover. Cover the pan and simmer for 30 minutes, or until the pears are tender and the sugar has completely dissolved. Allow the pears to cool, then transfer into sterilized jars, using a slotted spoon.

3 Boil the pear juice over a high heat until it has thickened and reduced to 240 ml (8 fl oz). Pour it over the pears. Pour in the brandy to within 2.5 cm (1 inch) of the tops.

4 Seal the jars and label. Keep in a cool dark place for at least 1 month before using, to allow the flavours to develop.

Fills about three 300 ml (10 fl oz) jars

COOK'S TIP To prevent discoloration, cover the peeled pears with lemon juice, or place in acidulated salted water made with 5 ml (1 tsp) salt and 5 ml (1 tsp) citric acid to each 1 litre (1¾ pints) water.

GRAPES IN WHISKY

INGREDIENTS

1–1.1 kg (2–2¼ lb) seedless grapes

450 g (1 lb) sugar

600–750 ml (1–1¼ pints) whisky

1 Prick the grapes all over with a sterilized needle or a wooden cocktail stick. Pack the grapes into sterilized jars, layering them with the sugar as you go. Leave about 2.5 cm (1 inch) space at the tops of the jars.

2 Slowly pour in the whisky to cover the grapes by 1.25 cm (½ inch), making sure that there are no air pockets.

3 Seal the jars, label, and shake well. Keep in a cool dark place for at least 2–3 months before using, to allow the flavours to develop. Shake from time to time during the first week of storage to make sure that all the sugar dissolves.

Fills about two 750 ml (1¼ pint) jars

PEARS IN RED WINE

INGREDIENTS

600 ml (1 pint) red wine

450 g (1 lb) sugar

2 kg (4½ lb) pears

2 cinnamon sticks

brandy

VARIATION The pears can be replaced by mixed soft red fruits, such as strawberries, raspberries, and redcurrants. Pack, uncooked, into sterilized jars. Prepare the red wine syrup as directed in step 1, adding 6 crushed cardamom pods. Strain the syrup and pour over the red fruits to cover.

1 Put the red wine and sugar into a preserving pan and stir over a low heat until the sugar has completely dissolved.

2 Peel, quarter, and core the pears, and add to the pan with the cinnamon sticks. Bring the mixture to a boil, lower the heat, and simmer the pears for 5–10 minutes, or until they are just tender. Take care not to overcook. Discard the cinnamon sticks. With a slotted spoon, transfer the pears to sterilized jars, to within 2.5 cm (1 inch) of the tops of the jars.

3 Increase the heat and boil the syrup rapidly, without stirring, for 5 minutes. Strain the syrup into a measuring jug and make up to 600–750 ml (1–1¼ pints) with brandy. Pour the mixture into the jars to cover the pears by 1.25 cm (½ inch). Seal the jars and label. Keep in a cool dark place for at least 2–3 months before using, to allow the flavours to develop.

Fills about two 750 ml (1¼ pint) jars

PAPAYAS IN RUM

INGREDIENTS

3 papayas

50 g (2 oz) pistachios

175 g (6 oz) sugar

325 ml (11 fl oz) rum

1 Peel and halve the papayas. Scoop out the seeds. Cut the flesh into large cubes. There should be about 575 g (1¼ lb) fruit.

2 Put the pistachios into a bowl and pour over boiling water to cover. Leave for 1 minute, then drain and transfer to a bowl of cold water. Drain again, then rub off the skins with your fingers.

3 Pack the papaya and pistachios into sterilized jars, layering them with the sugar as you go. Leave about 2.5 cm (1 inch) at the tops of the jars. Pour in the rum to cover the fruit and nuts by 1.25 cm (½ inch), making sure that there are no air pockets.

4 Seal the jars, label, and shake well. Keep in a cool dark place for at least 2–3 months before using, to allow the flavours to develop. Shake from time to time during the first week of storage to make sure that all the sugar dissolves.

Fills about two 600 ml (1 pint) jars

PINEAPPLES IN KIRSCH

INGREDIENTS

2 ripe pineapples, total weight
about 2 kg (4$^1/_2$ lb)

450 g (1 lb) sugar

450–600 ml ($^3/_4$–1 pint) kirsch

Kirsch is a cherry brandy which has a natural affinity with pineapple.

1 Slice the tops off the pineapples. Cut the peel off in strips, cutting deep enough to remove the "eyes" with the peel. Cut the pineapple across into thick slices, and cut out and discard the hard central core from each slice. Dice the flesh.

2 Pack the pineapple into sterilized jars, layering it with the sugar as you go. Leave about 2.5 cm (1 inch) space at the tops.

3 Pour in the kirsch to cover the pineapple by 1.25 cm ($^1/_2$ inch), making sure that there are no air pockets between the fruits. Seal the jars, label, and shake well.

4 Keep in a cool dark place for at least 1–2 months before using, to allow the flavours to develop. Shake from time to time during the first week of storage to make sure that all the sugar dissolves.

Fills about two 600 ml (1 pint) jars

RAISINS IN GENEVER WITH JUNIPER BERRIES

INGREDIENTS

675 g (1$^1/_2$ lb) raisins

350 g (12 oz) sugar

15 ml (1 tbsp) juniper berries

750–900 ml
(1$^1/_4$–1$^1/_2$ pints) genever gin

Gin is a spirit that is made from distilling juniper berries. It is therefore appropriate for gin and juniper to be mixed together in this recipe.

1 Layer the raisins with the sugar in sterilized jars, adding a few juniper berries with each layer.

2 Pour in the genever gin to cover the raisins, filling to the tops of the jars and making sure that there are no air pockets between the raisins. Seal the jars, label, and shake well.

3 The next day, check to see that the raisins have not risen above the level of the alcohol. If they have, remove a layer, and re-seal. Keep in a cool dark place for at least 2 months before using, to allow the flavours to develop. Shake from time to time during the first week of storage to make sure that all the sugar dissolves.

Fills about two 750 ml (1$^1/_4$ pint) jars

DID YOU KNOW?
Genever is a type of Dutch gin with a strong flavour. In Holland, raisins in genever are traditionally served in glasses on New Year's Eve. If you cannot get genever, ordinary gin can be used.

PEACHES IN BRANDY

INGREDIENTS

675 g–1 kg (1$^1/_2$–2 lb)
peaches, depending on size

350 g (12 oz) sugar

450–480 ml (15–16 fl oz)
brandy

1 Halve and stone the peaches. The fruits can also be peeled for a classic effect, but this is not necessary.

2 Pack the peach halves into sterilized jars, layering with the sugar as you go. Leave at least 2.5 cm (1 inch) at the tops of the jars.

3 Pour in the brandy to cover the peaches by 1.25 cm ($^1/_2$ inch), making sure that there are no air pockets between the fruits. Seal the jars, label, and shake well.

4 Keep in a cool dark place for at least 2–3 months before using, to allow the flavours to develop. Shake from time to time during the first week of storage to make sure that all the sugar dissolves.

Fills about two 900 ml (1$^1/_2$ pint) jars

FLAVOURED WINES & SPIRITS

ALMOST ALL commercially flavoured wines and spirits are made according to jealously guarded formulae. Aquavit with caraway seeds, gin with juniper berries, sambuca and ouzo with aniseed, to name but a few. Fruit brandies, known as *alcools blancs,* are commercially distilled from fresh fruits, the most popular being plums, Williams pears, black cherries, and raspberries, while the production of vermouths requires a complicated process involving herbs, sugar syrup, alcohol, and all manner of equipment.

Yet flavouring wines and spirits is not altogether out of reach of the home cook. Vanilla and cherry brandies are easy to make, while red hot chillies can transform the taste of sherry. Dry white wine is delicious when delicately flavoured with fruit, with the aid of a little sugar syrup. All it requires is enough patience to wait while the fruit and the wine exchange flavours. Although the wine will be the winner, the strained-out fruit can often be used, perhaps as an ingredient in a home-made ice cream or sorbet.

MAKING FLAVOURED WINES & SPIRITS

❦ Sterilize a large glass jar or bottle (see page 11) in which to steep the flavourings and alcohol.

❦ Choose the ingredients. Fresh berries and stone fruits are the best choice of fruits, and they should be ripe, but not over-ripe. Herbs and spices and other seasonings should be as fresh as possible. If flavouring with spice, use whole spices. The choice of alcohol depends on personal preference – any kind can be used, provided that it has an alcoholic content of at least 37.5% by volume.

❦ If fruits are being used as a flavouring, wash and dry them first. Remove any stalks, and any mouldy or damaged parts. Halve and stone fruits such as apricots. Cherries do not require stoning, but should be pricked all over with a sterilized needle or a wooden cocktail stick so that their flavour and colour can be released.

❦ Put the fruits into the prepared jar, layering it with sugar or pouring a sugar syrup over it, then add the alcohol. For herb- and spice-infused wines and spirits, simply insert the flavourings into sterilized bottles (lightly bruising fresh herbs first), and pour over the chosen alcohol.

❦ Allow the flavours to develop before using, shaking the bottles or jars from time to time. Allow about 3 months for fruit-infused spirits. Wines should be left to steep for 2–3 days if combined with fresh ingredients, and for up to 4 weeks if dried flavourings, such as apricots, herbs, and spices, are used.

❦ Strain the flavoured wine or spirit through a double layer of muslin into sterilized bottles.

How to seal and store
Seal the bottles tightly with non-corrosive screw-top lids or corks. Choose new corks, sterilize and secure them into the necks of the bottles with a wooden mallet. Spirits keep well and last almost indefinitely when stored in a cool dark place. Flavoured wines do not last as long. Once opened, the flavour will deteriorate after a few days, unless the wine has been combined with other preservatives (sugar and spirits).

What can go wrong and why
A flavoured wine or spirit will go cloudy if ground spices are used for flavouring. Always use whole spices. If the drink lacks flavour, the infusing time has been too short, or the ingredients are too bland.

CHERRY BRANDY

Traditionally, Morello cherries are used for this classic fruited spirit because they are less sweet than other varieties, but you can use any dark, flavoursome cherry instead. Let the brandy mature before decanting it into bottles, in time to give as a cheering winter gift. And don't neglect the cherries. After straining, they are delicious topped with fresh whipped cream.

INGREDIENTS

450 g (1 lb) cherries

75 g (3 oz) sugar

2 drops of almond essence

600 ml (1 pint) brandy

Fills one 1 litre (1³/₄ pint) bottle

1 ◄ Remove all the cherry stalks. Prick each cherry all over with a sterilized needle or a wooden cocktail stick.

2 ◄ Layer the cherries with the sugar in a large sterilized jar, to within 2.5 cm (1 inch) of the top. Add the almond essence to the jar.

3 ► Pour in the brandy to cover the cherries by 1.25 cm (¹/₂ inch). Seal the jar and shake well. Keep in a cool dark place for at least 3 months before using, to allow the flavours to develop. Shake the jar from time to time.

4 ► Line a funnel with a double layer of muslin and strain the brandy through it into a sterilized bottle. Seal the bottle and label. The brandy is now ready to use.

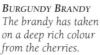

BURGUNDY BRANDY
The brandy has taken on a deep rich colour from the cherries.

Sloe Gin

Ingredients

450 g (1 lb) sloes

225 g (8 oz) sugar

1.15 litres (2 pints) gin

a few drops of almond essence (optional)

1 Remove any stalks from the sloes. Prick each sloe all over with a sterilized needle or a wooden cocktail stick.

2 Layer the sloes and sugar in a sterilized jar. Pour in the gin to cover the sloes completely and add the almond essence, if using. Seal the jar and shake well. Keep in a cool dark place for about 3 months before using, to allow the flavours to develop. Shake the jar from time to time.

3 Line a funnel with a double layer of muslin and strain the flavoured gin through it into sterilized bottles. Seal the bottles and label. The gin is now ready to use.

Makes about 1.15 litres (2 pints)

Apricot Wine with Brandy

Ingredients

100 g (4 oz) dried apricots

75 g (3 oz) sugar

1 bottle of dry white wine

30 ml (2 tbsp) brandy

1 Coarsely chop the apricots and put them into a saucepan with the sugar. Pour in just enough water to cover. Cover the pan and leave to stand for 2 hours. Simmer the apricots, stirring occasionally, for 10 minutes, or until the fruit is soft and tender.

2 Put the apricots and their syrup into a sterilized jar and slowly pour in the white wine and brandy to cover. Seal the jar and shake well, to remove any air pockets. Keep in a cool dark place for 3 weeks before using, to allow the flavours to develop. Shake the jar from time to time.

3 Line a funnel with a double layer of muslin and strain the flavoured wine through it into sterilized bottles. Seal the bottles and label. The wine is now ready to use.

Makes about 900 ml (1¹/₂ pints)

Cook's Tip Serve Apricot Wine with Brandy well chilled, as an aperitif. For a special occasion, pour it into a punch bowl and float nasturtium flowers on the top. The strained apricots can be served separately as a dessert, or as an accompaniment to savoury game, meat, or poultry dishes.

Blushing Strawberry Wine

Ingredients

225 g (8 oz) strawberries

3 sprigs of fresh lemon balm

1 sprig of fresh rosemary

1 sprig of fresh hyssop

1 bottle of semi-sweet rosé wine

This is a refreshing early summer drink which can be served either undiluted, or in tall glasses with a splash of sparkling water. Float vivid blue borage flowers or a sprig of lemon balm in each glass, for an attractive finish.

1 Hull and slice the strawberries. Lightly bruise the herbs to release their flavours. Put the strawberries and herbs into a sterilized jar and pour in the wine.

2 Seal the jar and shake well. Keep in a cool dark place for 2 days before using, to allow the flavours to develop. Shake the jar from time to time.

3 Line a funnel with a double layer of muslin and strain the flavoured wine through it into sterilized bottles. Seal the bottles, label, and keep in the refrigerator. The wine is now ready to use.

Makes about 900 ml (1¹/₂ pints)

Whisky Liqueur with Herbs

INGREDIENTS

225 g (8 oz) clear honey

900 ml (1½ pints) whisky

2 sprigs of dried fennel

2 sprigs of dried thyme

4 whole cloves

2 cinnamon sticks

1 Put the honey into a saucepan and heat just until warm. Remove from the heat and gradually stir in the whisky until the honey has completely dissolved. Transfer to a sterilized jar and add the herbs and spices. Seal the jar and shake well. Keep in a cool dark place for at least 4 months before using, to allow the flavours to develop. Shake the jar from time to time.

2 Line a funnel with a double layer of muslin and strain the flavoured whisky through it into sterilized bottles. Seal the bottles and label. The whisky is now ready to use.

Makes about 1 litre (1¾ pints)

Cassis

INGREDIENTS

450 g (1 lb) blackcurrants

600 ml (1 pint) dry white wine

about 675 g (1½ lb) sugar

about 300 ml (10 fl oz) brandy or gin

VARIATIONS Cassis is most commonly made with brandy or gin, but vodka can be used instead. A small cinnamon stick and a whole clove can be added to the syrup to give a touch of spice.

1 Lightly crush the blackcurrants in a large glass bowl. Stir in the wine, cover, and leave in a cool dark place for 2 days.

2 Blend the blackcurrant mixture in a food processor or blender. Line a large funnel with a double layer of muslin and strain the liquid through it. Measure the strained liquid. For each 300 ml (10 fl oz) liquid, weigh 225 g (8 oz) sugar. Put the liquid and sugar into a saucepan, and stir over a low heat until the sugar has completely dissolved. Do not boil. Simmer over a low heat, stirring occasionally, for 45 minutes.

3 Cool, then measure. For 3 parts blackcurrant syrup, add 1 part brandy or gin. Pour into sterilized bottles. Seal the bottles and label. Keep in a cool dark place for 2–3 days before using, to allow the flavours to develop.

Makes about 1.15 litres (2 pints)

Hot Pepper Sherry or Rum

INGREDIENTS

6 hot red chillies, fresh or dried

600 ml (1 pint) dry sherry or light rum

This is a potent brew, so add a few drops sparingly to stews or sauces.

1 Put the chillies into a sterilized bottle with the sherry or rum. Seal and shake well. Keep in a cool dark place for 2 weeks before using, to allow the flavours to develop. Shake the bottle from time to time. Remove the chillies before using.

Makes about 600 ml (1 pint)

Vanilla Brandy

INGREDIENTS

2 whole vanilla pods

600 ml (1 pint) brandy

*STRAWBERRY SURPRISE
Blushing Strawberry
Wine is glamorized with
borage flowers.*

1 Cut the vanilla pods lengthwise to release their flavour. Put them into a sterilized bottle with the brandy. Seal, label, and shake well. Keep in a cool dark place for 3 weeks before using, to allow the flavours to develop. Shake the bottle from time to time.

2 Remove the vanilla pods. The brandy is now ready to use.

Makes about 600 ml (1 pint)

FRUIT CORDIALS & SYRUPS

QUENCH A SUMMER THIRST with a non-alcoholic fruit cordial or syrup diluted with soda, water, lemonade even. A syrup or cordial is often the base for an alcohol punch or cocktail. A single fruit can be used for a syrup, but any fruits can be combined in a recipe as long as some of them are sour enough to balance the sweetness of the sugar. Too sweet a taste would lack the refreshing tartness that makes these drinks such ideal companions for hot sunny days. However, these drinks are welcome at any time, thirst knows no season.

The cordials and syrups are concentrated, and a little goes a long way, so they are economical when made in quantity, especially if you are able to pick your own wild fruits for free. The best fruits are juicy berries, such as strawberries, raspberries, loganberries, and blackberries. Citrus fruits are good too: utilize both zest and pulp to maximize the citrus flavour. Even exotic tropical fruits make ideal ingredients for cordials and syrups, with kiwi fruit, passion fruit, kumquats, and pineapples giving a subtly fragrant flavour.

MAKING FRUIT CORDIALS & SYRUPS

❧ Choose the fruits. Fully ripe or even slightly over-ripe fruits with plenty of flavour are best for cordials and syrups. Granulated sugar is usual choice of sweetener. Make sure you have enough sugar available before you start, because the exact amount is often calculated after the juice has been extracted from the fruits.

❧ Prepare the fruits; discard any mouldy or damaged parts, and wash and dry them, as necessary. Then extract the juice. This is done by lightly heating, pressing, or squeezing them. The aim is to do this without destroying the flavour, so do not overcook the fruits.

❧ Strain the fruit purée through a double layer of muslin, then lightly squeeze it to extract as much juice as possible.

❧ Add sugar to the juice and dissolve over a very low heat. The mixture is then boiled for about 5 minutes.

❧ Leave the mixture to cool, then pour into sterilized bottles (see page 11), to within 3 mm (1/8 inch) of the tops.

How to seal and store
Seal tightly with screw-top lids or plastic stoppers. Corks can also be used (see Flavoured Vinegars, page 117). The recipes in this section do not include any special heat treatments nor do they contain sufficient sugar to allow for long storage, so the cordials and syrups should be drunk straightaway, or kept in the refrigerator for only 3–4 weeks. Alternatively, they can be frozen. A convenient way to freeze them is in ice-cube trays: pour in the drink, leaving room for it to expand. When frozen, turn the cubes out into plastic bags and keep in the freezer. One ice cube will be enough for a 240 ml (8 fl oz) drink, ideal for making in a hurry.

What can go wrong and why
If a cordial or syrup develops a sediment at the bottom of the bottle it is merely tiny pieces of pulp that have slipped through during straining. Simply pour the cordial or syrup with care so that the sediment is not disturbed.

PINEAPPLE AND LIME SYRUP

This syrup has a taste of the tropics, making it a wonderful base for rum punches and daiquiries. Alternatively, serve it diluted with a little sparkling water as a cooling non-alcoholic drink. Lots of ice cubes and fresh twists of citrus zest will give it added zip.

INGREDIENTS

2 pineapples, total weight about 2 kg (4½ lb)

300 ml (10 fl oz) water

about 175 g (6 oz) sugar

juice of 3 limes

Makes about 600 ml (1 pint)

1 ▶ Slice the tops off the pineapples. Cut off the peel in strips, cutting deep enough to remove the "eyes". Slice the pineapple, and cut out and discard the hard central core from each slice; finely chop the flesh.

2 ▼ Put the pineapple into a saucepan with the water and bring to a boil. Simmer over a low heat for 20 minutes, or until the fruit is soft and pulpy. Mash with a potato masher.

3 ▼ Line a plastic sieve with a double layer of muslin. Strain the pulp through it into a bowl. Gather the corners of the muslin and lightly squeeze to extract all the juice possible. Discard the pulp. Measure the juice. For each 300 ml (10 fl oz) juice, weigh 100 g (4 oz) sugar.

ZESTY FINISH
Juicy limes add a refreshing tang to pineapple syrup.

4 ▶ Pour the juice back into the saucepan, add the sugar, and stir over a low heat until the sugar has completely dissolved. Stir in the lime juice.

5 Bring the mixture to a boil and simmer over a low heat for 5 minutes. Cool for 5 minutes, then pour into sterilized bottles, to within 3 mm (⅛ inch) of the tops. Seal the bottles, label, and keep in the refrigerator. The syrup is now ready to use.

STRAWBERRY SYRUP

INGREDIENTS

1.4 kg (3 lb) strawberries

sugar

juice of 2 lemons

1 Hull the strawberries and purée them in a food processor. Line a plastic sieve with a double layer of muslin. Strain the pulp through it into a non-metallic bowl. Gather the corners of the muslin and lightly squeeze to extract all the juice possible.

2 Measure the juice. For each 600 ml (1 pint) juice, weigh 350 g (12 oz) sugar. Pour the juice into a saucepan, add the sugar, and stir over a low heat until the sugar has completely dissolved. Stir in the lemon juice. Cool for 5 minutes.

3 Pour into sterilized bottles, to within 3 mm ($^1/_8$ inch) of the tops. Seal the bottles, label, and keep in the refrigerator.

Makes about 1 litre (1$^3/_4$ pints)

VARIATIONS
Other strongly acidic fruits, such as raspberries, can be used to make this syrup. Blackcurrants can be used, in which case, add 900 ml (1$^1/_2$ pints) water while syrup is cooling.

LOGANBERRY AND LEMON BALM CORDIAL

INGREDIENTS

1.8 kg (4 lb) loganberries

4 sprigs of lemon balm

600 ml (1 pint) water

sugar

juice of 2 lemons

1 Put the loganberries and the lemon balm into a large saucepan with the water, and bring to a boil. Simmer over a low heat for 8–10 minutes, until the fruit is soft. Mash with a potato masher.

2 Line a plastic sieve with a double layer of muslin. Strain the pulp through it into a non-metallic bowl. Gather the corners of the muslin and lightly squeeze to extract all the juice possible.

3 Measure the juice. For each 600 ml (1 pint) juice, weigh 225 g (8 oz) sugar. Pour the juice back into the saucepan, add the sugar, and stir over a low heat until the sugar has completely dissolved. Stir in the lemon juice. Bring the mixture to a boil and simmer for 5 minutes. Cool for 5 minutes.

4 Pour into sterilized bottles, to within 3 mm ($^1/_8$ inch) of the tops. Seal the bottles, label, and keep in the refrigerator.

Makes about 1 litre (1$^3/_4$ pints)

KUMQUAT CORDIAL

INGREDIENTS

450 g (1 lb) kumquats

300 ml (10 fl oz) water

juice of 10 oranges, about 750 ml (1$^1/_4$ pints)

sugar

1 Slice the kumquats and put the slices into a saucepan with the water. Bring to a boil and simmer for 30 minutes, until the fruit is very soft.

2 Line a plastic sieve with a double layer of muslin. Strain the pulp through it into a non-metallic bowl. Gather the corners of the muslin and lightly squeeze to extract all the juice possible.

3 Mix the kumquat juice with the orange juice. Measure the total amount of juice. For each 600 ml (1 pint) juice, weigh 225 g (8 oz) sugar. Pour the juice back into the saucepan, add the sugar, and stir over a low heat until the sugar has completely dissolved. Cool for 5 minutes.

4 Pour into sterilized bottles, to within 3 mm ($^1/_8$ inch) of the tops. Seal the bottles, label, and keep in the refrigerator.

Makes about 1 litre (1$^3/_4$ pints)

ST. CLEMENT'S CORDIAL

INGREDIENTS

juice of 8 oranges, about 750 ml (1¼ pints)

juice of 6 lemons, about 350 ml (12 fl oz)

finely grated zest of 2 oranges and 2 lemons

1 kg (2 lb) sugar

Serve this cordial with an equal amount of iced, still, or sparkling water.

1 Put the juice and grated zest into a saucepan. Add the sugar and stir over a low heat until the sugar has completely dissolved. Increase the heat and bring to just below boiling point. Immediately remove from the heat. Leave to cool completely.

2 Line a plastic sieve with a double layer of muslin. Strain the pulp through it into a non-metallic bowl. Gather the corners of the muslin and lightly squeeze to extract all the juice possible. Pour into sterilized bottles, to within 3 mm (⅛ inch) of the tops. Seal the bottles, label, and keep in the refrigerator.

Makes about 1.4 litres (2½ pints)

BLACKBERRY AND APPLE CORDIAL

INGREDIENTS

1.8 kg (4 lb) blackberries

600 ml (1 pint) apple juice

sugar

juice of 2 lemons

1 Put the blackberries into a large saucepan with the apple juice. Bring to a boil and simmer over a very low heat for 20 minutes, or until the fruit is soft. Mash with a potato masher. Line a plastic sieve with a double layer of muslin. Strain the pulp through it into a non-metallic bowl. Gather the corners of the muslin and lightly squeeze to extract all the juice possible.

2 Measure the juice. For each 600 ml (1 pint) juice, weigh 225 g (8 oz) sugar. Pour the juice back into the saucepan, add the sugar, and stir over a low heat until the sugar has completely dissolved. Stir in the lemon juice. Bring the mixture to a boil and simmer for 5 minutes. Cool for 5 minutes.

3 Pour into sterilized bottles, to within 3 mm (⅛ inch) of the tops. Seal the bottles, label, and keep in the refrigerator.

Makes about 1 litre (1¾ pints)

KIWI-PASSION FRUIT SYRUP

INGREDIENTS

1 kg (2 lb) kiwi fruit

8 passion fruit

sugar

These fragrant tropical fruits are delicious when combined together.

1 Peel and coarsely chop the kiwi fruit. Halve the passion fruit, scoop out the seeds and flesh, and discard the skins. Purée the flesh of both fruits in a food processor or blender.

2 Line a plastic sieve with a double layer of muslin. Strain the pulp through it into a non-metallic bowl. Gather the corners of the muslin and lightly squeeze to extract all the juice possible.

3 Measure the juice. For each 150 ml (5 fl oz) juice, weigh 225 g (8 oz) sugar. Pour the juice into a saucepan, add the sugar, and stir over a low heat until the sugar has completely dissolved. Bring to a boil and simmer for 5 minutes. Cool for 5 minutes.

4 Pour into sterilized bottles, to within 3 mm (⅛ inch) of the tops. Seal the bottles, label, and keep in the refrigerator.

Makes about 600 ml (1 pint)

PASSION FRUIT PULP
Use a small teaspoon to extract the yellow pulp and crunchy black seeds from the passion fruit.

PICKLES, CHUTNEYS, RELISHES & MUSTARDS

VEGETABLE & FRUIT PICKLES

PICKLING IS the perfect answer to nature's exuberant harvest. Fruits and vegetables can be "put up" in jars and bottles to give a fillip to foods, adding a sharp and spicy accent to ordinary winter fare. The jewel-like colours of ruby beetroots, emerald green beans, and moonstone-shaped garlic cloves make attractive pickles. Fruit pickles can be made from hard or fleshy fruits like apples, peaches, pears, and melons. Probably the most famous vegetable pickles are pickled onions, and cucumber or dill pickles. Pickled onions are a favourite for a pub-type lunch with bread and cheese and a tankard of beer or ale. More unusual is pickled garlic, gentled by vinegar, which makes an interesting nibble with drinks.

Pickles have always played an important part in many other cuisines, particularly those of the Middle and Far East. To the pickle-loving Japanese, any meal without pickles is simply incomplete. A favourite of theirs is pickled ginger, which takes little time to prepare, but is infinitely useful as a garnish. Everyone has a list of favourite foods they like to pickle. Oranges, dates, and cherries make exceedingly luxurious pickles, and spiced cranberries enchant with their exquisite pink colour as well as their tart flavour. Green tomato pickles, pickled sweet red peppers, courgettes flavoured with seeds and spices, or carrots scented with thyme and coriander and sweetened with sugar – the combination of foods for pickling seems almost endless.

MAKING VEGETABLE & FRUIT PICKLES

❦ Select the ingredients. Vinegar, added to prevent spoilage by micro-organisms, is the main ingredient for preserving pickles. Use only best-quality bottled vinegar. Most brands of vinegar have an acetic acid content of 5–7 per cent. Avoid draught vinegar, which may have an acetic acid content of less than 5 per cent. Malt vinegar is the most economical vinegar for pickling. Although its flavour is quite potent, it is the best vinegar for general pickling purposes. Cider and wine vinegar may be recommended where the spicing is more delicate, or when a lighter colour is desired. Spiced Pickling Vinegar (see recipe, page 120) gives a good flavour to pickles. For a more sophisticated taste, vinegars flavoured with herbs or fruits can be used (see Flavoured Vinegars, pages 117–121). The general rule when choosing vinegar, is to match the vinegar to suit the type of vegetable or fruit you are pickling, and to consider the overall colour and flavour you want to create.

❦ Salt, which may be used for salting vegetables before pickling is another essential preservative for many pickles. Choose sea salt, never table salt which contains chemical additives to keep it free-flowing. Sometimes the vinegar is sweetened; granulated sugar is the usual choice for this, but brown sugars of various kinds may be used for their flavour in certain spiced pickles. Many pickling recipes call for spices: use whole spices because they are easily removed and will also give a clear pickling liquid. Ground spices will cloud the vinegar.

❦ There is no real restriction on the type of vegetables that can be used in pickles, as long as they are firm, even-sized, young, and fresh. If pickling whole items, choose small sizes for easier packing. The most popular pickles are made with beetroots, onions, red and white cabbages, cauliflower, cucumbers, and a mixture of different vegetables. Mushrooms, artichokes, and peppers also make excellent pickles. Choose fruits that are not over-ripe and are as fresh as possible. Fruits such as melons, peaches, pears, and plums are usually pickled in sweetened vinegar, whereas lemons can be pickled in salt.

❧ Prepare the vegetables or fruits. Using a stainless steel knife, peel and trim the vegetables or fruits as appropriate. Remove any mouldy or damaged parts. If cooking is required, steam the vegetables or cook the fruits in a light syrup.

❧ Some raw vegetables need to be salted or brined before they are pickled. This is to extract the moisture they contain so the vinegar can penetrate the food and preserve it. (Cooked fruits and vegetables do not need to be brined because the cooking process boils off excess water.) The recipe may stipulate dry-brining or wet-brining. For dry-brining, the vegetables are layered with salt in a large non-metallic bowl, left to stand overnight, and stirred occasionally. For wet-brining, a solution of salt and water is poured over the vegetables, which are again left to stand overnight, and stirred occasionally. After brining, the vegetables must be drained, washed, and drained again to remove all the salt, then patted dry with kitchen paper. Avoid using any metal utensils when brining.

❧ Pack the brined or cooked fruits or vegetables into dry sterilized jars (see page 11). Do not pack too tightly, because you need to leave space for the vinegar to surround them. Instead of packing single vegetables separately, layering different vegetables in the same jar can create a decorative effect. Cooked vegetables can be left to stand for an hour in the jars so that any liquid which collects at the bottom can be drained off before proceeding.

❧ Cover the vegetables with vinegar, tapping the jars to prevent air pockets from forming. Fruits are pickled in hot syrup or vinegar or a mixture of both. Leave at least 1.25 cm (½ inch) space at the top of the jar after packing the fruits or vegetables. The vinegar can then be poured in almost to the tops of the jars – ensuring the fruits are well covered – even if some of it evaporates during storage.

❧ Some pickles have a tendency to float to the tops of the jars. This can be overcome by putting a piece of crumpled greaseproof paper in the top of the jar above the pickles. Remove after a couple of weeks when the pickles should remain submerged.

How to seal and store

Seal the pickles tightly with non-corrosive, screw-top lids. Pickles should be stored in a cool dark place, such as a cupboard, which is dry and well-ventilated. Vegetable pickles are usually ready to eat after 2–3 weeks, but pickled fruits should be left for about 2 months before using, to allow the flavours to develop. Pickled vegetables and fruits that are covered with pure vinegar will last longer than those which are covered with a combination of water or oil and vinegar. If the vinegar evaporates during storage, top up with more so that the food is always covered.

What can go wrong and why

Yellow spots sometimes appear on pickled onions. This is due to the formation of a harmless substance, and the onions can still be eaten despite their appearance. Certain vegetables, such as courgettes, will have a bitter taste if they are not brined or salted before they are pickled. If pickles do not keep well, it could be because they were not brined for long enough, which means that too much moisture came out of them during storage and diluted the vinegar. Alternatively, the vinegar may not have been up to strength and contained less than 5% acetic acid, which helps to preserve the pickles. Too short a salting or brining time can also make the vinegar cloudy. If the pickles become soft, they may have been left too long before eating. Air pockets will be trapped in the jars if the vegetables or fruits are packed too tightly, and the vinegar has not been able to completely surround them. Gently tapping the jars once they are filled will help remove any pockets that do form. Pickles will go mouldy on top if they are not fully covered with vinegar when being bottled. If the jars are not sealed correctly, vinegar will evaporate, causing the contents of the jars to shrink and dry out. If the lids used are not non-corrosive, then rust will form and it will contaminate the pickles.

> **DID YOU KNOW?** The idea of pickling vegetables and fruits is not a new one. In fact it is one of the most ancient forms of preserving foods, dating back to Greek and Roman times. The Romans had the advantage of having an extensive variety of foods to pickle, which they imported from the lands they conquered in Europe. Onions, lemons, plums, and peaches, as well as herbs, roots, and flowers, would all probably have fallen prey to the large pickling vases used as storage vessels. These were steeped in a mixture of vinegar, oil, and brine, sometimes honey, not unlike the pickles we make today.

EQUIPMENT

Pickles, chutneys, relishes, and mustards use readily available pieces of kitchen equipment, similar to those needed for jams and other preserves. Just a few different utensils are necessary.

Large non-metallic bowls are needed for brining and salting, the initial process in many pickle recipes which helps extract excess water from the vegetables. Everyday china or glass plates can be used to hold the vegetables or fruits down in the brining solution. Kitchen paper is then required to dry the ingredients once they have been rinsed and drained in a plastic colander or sieve. Metal bowls, plates, and sieves should be avoided, particularly if they are to come into contact with vinegar, because vinegar will corrode them and give the pickle a disagreeable taste. Small stainless steel pans are ideal for heating vinegars and vinegar syrups. Chutneys and relishes are best made in a good-quality stainless steel preserving pan. Make sure it is spotless and that the pan is neither pitted nor buckled. Avoid brass or copper preserving pans, because the vinegar will corrode them.

If whole spices are to be added to the mixture, but need to be removed later, a piece of muslin is most useful for tying them into a bag. Use a double thickness of muslin and secure to the pan handle with a long piece of string, so that the bag can be lifted out easily.

Greaseproof paper is often used in pickles to keep the ingredients under the level of the vinegar, and this should be removed after 1–2 weeks storage. Although ingredients, such as sugar and salt, used in making pickles, chutneys, relishes, and mustards, are to some degree natural preservatives, using sterilized containers and lids for storage will also protect against spoilage. Make sure that glass jars are as clean as possible, not cracked, and can be made airtight with non-corrosive, screw-top lids.

PICKLED ONIONS

INGREDIENTS

1–1.15 kg (2–2¹/₂ lb) pickling onions, depending on size

100 g (4 oz) sea salt

1.15 litres (2 pints) water

750 ml (1¹/₄ pints) strained Spiced Pickling Vinegar (see recipe, page 120)

In this recipe, special pickling onions have been used, but you can use shallots instead if you prefer.

1 Trim and peel the onions, leaving a little of the root attached so that they remain whole and do not fall apart. Put them into a large non-metallic bowl.

2 Dissolve the salt in the water and pour over the onions. Cover and leave to stand for 24 hours, stirring from time to time.

3 Rinse the onions in a plastic sieve or colander under cold running water. Drain well and dry on kitchen paper.

4 Pack the onions into sterilized jars, to within 2.5 cm (1 inch) of the tops. Pour in the vinegar, to cover them by 1.25 cm (¹/₂ inch). Gently tap the jars to remove any air pockets.

5 Seal the jars and label. Keep in a cool dark place for 3 weeks before using, to allow the flavours to develop.

COOK'S TIP If the vegetables in any of these recipes show a tendency to float, put crumpled greaseproof paper in the top of the jar to hold the vegetables under the liquid. Remove the paper after 1 week.

Fills about three 300 ml (10 fl oz) jars

PICKLED HORSERADISH

INGREDIENTS

175 g (6 oz) fresh horseradish

350 ml (12 fl oz) strained Spiced Pickling Vinegar (see recipe, page 120)

75 g (3 oz) sugar

5 ml (1 tsp) sea salt

1 Peel and finely grate the horseradish, then check the weight. You should have 100 g (4 oz) grated horseradish.

2 Put the vinegar, sugar, and salt into a saucepan and bring to a boil. Stir over a low heat, with a wooden spoon, until the sugar has completely dissolved, then boil for 2 minutes. Add the horseradish and simmer for 1 minute.

3 Pack the horseradish and vinegar mixture into warmed sterilized jars, to within 3 mm (¹/₈ inch) of the tops.

4 Seal the jars and label. Keep in a cool dark place for 1 week before using, to allow the flavours to develop.

Fills about two 175 ml (6 fl oz) jars

MOROCCAN PICKLED PEPPERS

INGREDIENTS

1 kg (2 lb) red and green peppers

50 g (2 oz) sea salt

2 small heads of garlic

300 ml (10 fl oz) olive oil

300 ml (10 fl oz) white wine vinegar

1 Cut around the core of each pepper and pull it out. Quarter each pepper, scrape out the seeds, and cut away the white ribs. Sprinkle the inside of each quarter liberally with the salt.

2 Peel the garlic cloves. Mix the olive oil and wine vinegar together. Pack the peppers and garlic, in layers, into a sterilized jar, to within 2.5 cm (1 inch) of the top.

3 Pour in the oil and vinegar mixture, to cover the peppers and garlic by 1.25 cm (¹/₂ inch).

4 Gently tap the jar to remove any air pockets. Seal the jar and label. Keep in the refrigerator and use within 1–2 weeks.

Fills one 1.25 litre (2¹/₄ pint) jar

MIXED VEGETABLE PICKLES

A variety of crisp vegetables look attractive when neatly layered in a tall jar and covered with Spiced Pickling Vinegar. Use them to create a colourful winter salad, or as an accompaniment to creamy dips.

INGREDIENTS

450 g (1 lb) green beans

450 g (1 lb) small pickling onions

1 small cauliflower, weighing about 350 g (12 oz)

350 g (12 oz) courgettes

225 g (8 oz) peeled carrots

100 g (4 oz) sea salt

450 ml (15 fl oz) strained Spiced Pickling Vinegar (see recipe, page 120)

Fills one 1.15 litre (2 pint) jar and one 600 ml (1 pint) jar

Make sure the vegetables are well covered with vinegar

1 ▲ Trim the beans and cut them into neat 2.5 cm (1 inch) lengths. Trim and peel the onions, leaving them whole, but with a little root attached so that they do not fall apart. Cut the florets from the cauliflower and break into 1.25 cm (1/2 inch) pieces. Trim the courgettes and carrots and cut them into 3 mm (1/8 inch) thick slices.

2 ▶ Layer the vegetables with the salt in a large non-metallic bowl. Put a plate on top to keep the vegetables lightly pressed down, and leave for 24–48 hours, to draw out the excess moisture.

3 Rinse the vegetables in a plastic sieve or colander under cold running water until all the salt is washed off. Drain the vegetables well and dry on kitchen paper.

4 Neatly pack the vegetables in separate layers into sterilized jars, to within 2.5 cm (1 inch) of the tops.

5 ▲ Pour in the pickling vinegar, to cover the vegetables by 1.25 cm (1/2 inch). Gently tap the jars to remove any air pockets. Seal the jars and label. Keep in a cool dark place for 6 weeks before using, to allow the flavours to develop.

PICKLED BABY VEGETABLES

INGREDIENTS

1.15 kg (2¹/2 lb) mixed baby vegetables

100 g (4 oz) sea salt

800 ml (28 fl oz) strained Spiced Pickling Vinegar (see recipe, page 120)

PICKLED JERUSALEM ARTICHOKES Do not salt and leave to stand overnight, but simmer in 600 ml (1 pint) salted water until tender. Drain, cool, and dry, then continue from step 3.

Choose baby vegetables which will maintain their crispness during pickling. Carrots, sweetcorn, and mangetout are possible choices.

1 Trim all the vegetables and peel, if necessary. Layer the vegetables with the salt in a large non-metallic bowl. Put a plate on top to keep them lightly pressed down, and leave to stand overnight, to draw out the excess moisture.

2 Rinse the vegetables in a plastic sieve or colander under cold running water. Drain well and dry on kitchen paper.

3 Pack the vegetables into sterilized jars, to within 2.5 cm (1 inch) of the tops. Pour in the pickling vinegar, to cover the vegetables by 1.25 cm (¹/2 inch). Gently tap the jars to remove air pockets.

4 Seal the jars and label. Keep in a cool dark place for 4 weeks before using, to allow the flavours to develop.

Fills about two 900 ml (1¹/2 pint) jars

DILL PICKLES WITH GARLIC

INGREDIENTS

3 large garlic cloves

10–12 pickling cucumbers

1 bunch of fresh dill about 7 g (¹/4 oz)

600 ml (1 pint) water

900 ml (1¹/2 pints) white wine vinegar

75 g (3 oz) sea salt

10 ml (2 tsp) Pickling Spice (see recipe, page 126)

5 ml (1 tsp) dill seeds

5 ml (1 tsp) black peppercorns

There are many recipes for dill pickles, which are also known as kosher pickles. In this recipe water is mixed with vinegar to make a mild pickle. Other flavourings can also be used, such as onions, fennel, or cloves.

1 Peel the garlic cloves and pack them into a sterilized jar with the cucumbers and sprigs of dill.

2 Pour the water and vinegar into a saucepan and add the salt, pickling spice, dill seeds, and peppercorns. Bring to a boil, and boil rapidly for 3 minutes. Leave to cool.

3 Pour the cooled mixture over the cucumbers, to cover them by 1.25 cm (¹/2 inch). If there is too much liquid, add any remaining spices to the jar and discard the excess liquid.

4 Seal the jar and label. Keep in the refrigerator for 3 weeks before using, to allow the flavours to develop.

5 After a day or two, check that the cucumbers are still well covered. If they are protruding out of the vinegar, push them down into the liquid and hold them down with a crumpled piece of greaseproof paper. Remove the paper after 2 weeks.

Fills one 2 litre (3¹/2 pint) jar

VARIATION Instead of leaving the cucumbers whole, thinly slice them and layer them in sterilized jars, with 2 peeled and sliced onions, 2 peeled garlic cloves, and the dill. Continue as for whole cucumbers.

PICKLED CAULIFLOWER WITH PEPPERS

INGREDIENTS

2 cauliflowers

1 red pepper

150 g (5 oz) sea salt

900 ml (1½ pints) water

1 cinnamon stick, broken into 3 pieces

3 blades of mace

900 ml (1½ pints) strained Spiced Pickling Vinegar (see recipe, page 120)

1 Cut the florets from the cauliflowers and discard the stalks. Put the florets into a large non-metallic bowl. Core, seed, and dice the pepper and add to the bowl with the cauliflower.

2 Dissolve the salt in the water and pour over the vegetables. Weight down with a plate to keep the vegetables submerged. Leave to stand for 24 hours.

3 Rinse the cauliflower and pepper in a plastic sieve or colander under cold running water. Drain well and dry on kitchen paper.

4 Pack the vegetables into sterilized jars, to within 2.5 cm (1 inch) of the tops, adding a piece of cinnamon stick and a blade of mace to each jar. Pour in the pickling vinegar, to cover the vegetables by 1.25 cm (½ inch).

5 Seal the jars and label. Keep in a cool dark place for 4 weeks before using, to allow the flavours to develop.

Fills about three 300 ml (10 fl oz) jars

COURGETTE PICKLES

INGREDIENTS

1.4 kg (3 lb) courgettes

450 g (1 lb) onions

225 g (8 oz) sea salt

2.5 litres (4½ pints) water

450 ml (15 fl oz) white malt vinegar

225 g (8 oz) sugar

10 ml (2 tsp) mustard seeds

5 ml (1 tsp) celery seeds

5 ml (1 tsp) whole allspice

1 Trim the courgettes and peel and trim the onions. Slice both vegetables thinly and place them in a large non-metallic bowl.

2 Dissolve the salt in the water and pour over the vegetables. Leave to stand for 3 hours, stirring from time to time.

3 Mix all the remaining ingredients in a saucepan. Stir over a low heat, with a wooden spoon, until the sugar has completely dissolved.

4 Rinse the courgettes and onions in a plastic sieve or colander under cold running water. Drain well and dry on kitchen paper. Put into a preserving pan. Pour the hot vinegar over the vegetables and leave to stand, off the heat, for 1 hour.

5 Put the pan over a medium heat, and bring to a boil. Boil for 3 minutes, then remove from the heat.

6 Transfer the vegetables to warmed sterilized jars, to within 2.5 cm (1 inch) of the tops. Pour in the vinegar, to cover by 1.25 cm (½ inch). Seal the jars and label. Keep in a cool dark place for 2 weeks before using, to allow the flavours to develop.

Fills about two 750 ml (1¼ pint) jars

SWEET PEPPER PICKLES

Peppers offer a riot of colour when used in making pickles. Extra flavour comes from slivers of sun-dried tomatoes, and spiced vinegar which has a hint of sweetness. Serve these pickles with cold meats or on an antipasto platter.

INGREDIENTS

4 large peppers (red, green, orange, and yellow)

1 onion

175 g (6 oz) sea salt

350 ml (12 fl oz) strained Spiced Pickling Vinegar (see recipe, page 120)

50 g (2 oz) sugar

25 g (1 oz) sun-dried tomatoes

Fills one 1.15 litre (2 pint) jar

1 ◀ Cut around the core of each pepper and pull it out. Halve each pepper lengthwise and scrape out the seeds. Cut away the white ribs on the inside. Cut each half lengthwise into 3 mm (⅛ inch) wide strips. Peel and finely chop the onion.

2 Layer the peppers, onion, and salt in a large non-metallic bowl. Put a plate on top to keep the vegetables lightly pressed down, and leave for 24 hours, covered, to draw out the excess moisture. Toss from time to time.

3 Rinse the vegetables in a plastic sieve or colander under cold running water, until all the salt is washed off. Drain and dry on kitchen paper.

4 Gently heat the pickling vinegar and sugar in a small saucepan, stirring until the sugar has completely dissolved. Cool.

6 ▲ Cut the tomatoes into thin shreds. Mix with the other vegetables and pack them into a sterilized jar, to within 2.5 cm (1 inch) of the top. Pour in the vinegar, to cover the vegetables by 1.25 cm (½ inch). Gently tap the jar to remove any air pockets.

5 Put the sun-dried tomatoes into a bowl and cover with boiling water. Leave for 5 minutes, then drain well.

7 Seal the jar and label. Keep in a cool dark place for 6 weeks before using, to allow the flavours to develop.

SWEET AND SOUR CARROTS

INGREDIENTS

1 kg (2 lb) small carrots

100 g (4 oz) sea salt

2 garlic cloves

300 ml (10 fl oz) white wine
vinegar

100 g (4 oz) dark soft brown
sugar

10 ml (2 tsp) ground
cinnamon

5 ml (1 tsp) ground coriander

5 ml (1 tsp) dried thyme

1 small dried red chilli

These oriental-style carrots can be served on a platter of mixed hors d'oeuvre. Olives, artichoke hearts, and marinated peppers are excellent accompaniments.

1 Peel and thinly slice the carrots. Layer them with the salt in a large non-metallic bowl. Put a plate on top to keep the carrots lightly pressed down, and leave for 24 hours, covered, to draw out the excess moisture. Toss from time to time.

2 Peel the garlic cloves and put them into a saucepan with all the remaining ingredients. Stir over a low heat until the sugar has completely dissolved. Remove from the heat and leave the mixture to stand until required.

3 Rinse the carrots in a plastic sieve or colander under cold running water, until all the salt is washed off. Drain and dry on kitchen paper.

4 Pack the carrots into sterilized jars, to within 2.5 cm (1 inch) of the tops. Slowly pour in the vinegar, to cover the carrots by 1.25 cm ($^1/_2$ inch). Gently tap the jars to remove any air pockets.

5 Seal the jars and label. Keep in a cool dark place for 1 week before using, to allow the flavours to develop.

Fills about two 350 ml (12 fl oz) jars

PICKLED RED CABBAGE

INGREDIENTS

1 small red cabbage, weighing
about 1.15 kg (2$^1/_2$ lb)

75 g (3 oz) sea salt

5 ml (1 tsp) sugar

300 ml (10 fl oz) strained
Spiced Pickling Vinegar
(see recipe, page 120)

1 Remove any discoloured outer leaves from the cabbage. Cut the cabbage into quarters, and discard the tough central core. Shred the cabbage finely.

2 Layer the cabbage with the salt in a large non-metallic bowl. Put a plate on top to keep the cabbage lightly pressed down, and leave for 24 hours, covered, to draw out the excess moisture.

3 Rinse the cabbage in a plastic sieve or colander under cold running water, until all the salt is washed off. Drain and dry on kitchen paper.

4 Pack the cabbage into sterilized jars, sprinkling with a little sugar as you go, to within 2.5 cm (1 inch) of the tops. Slowly pour in the pickling vinegar, to cover the cabbage by 1.25 cm ($^1/_2$ inch). Gently tap the jars to remove any air pockets.

5 Seal the jars and label. Keep in a cool dark place for 2–3 weeks before using, to allow the flavours to develop.

Fills about two 600 ml (1 pint) jars

VARIATION
A quick version of Pickled Red Cabbage can be made if the red cabbage is not salted. However, it will not remain as crisp, and must be eaten within 2–3 months.

PICKLED DICED BEETROOT

INGREDIENTS

1 kg (2 lb) uncooked beetroots

5 ml (1 tsp) sea salt

5 ml (1 tsp) freshly grated
horseradish (optional)

1.15 litres (2 pints) white
wine vinegar

This recipe is for cubes of beetroot. If slices are preferred, follow the recipe as directed and, when the beetroots are cool, peel and slice them. Pack the slices into sterilized jars and fill with cold vinegar.

1 Wash the beetroots, taking care not to damage their skins.

2 Put the beetroots into a large saucepan and cover with water. Add the salt. Simmer, covered, for $1^1/_2$–2 hours, or until the beetroots are tender. Do not pierce them to test or the beetroots will "bleed" and lose their colour. Leave to cool.

3 Peel the beetroots, and cut into dice. Pack the diced beetroot into sterilized jars, with the horseradish if using, to within 2.5 cm (1 inch) of the tops.

4 Put the vinegar into a pan and bring to a boil. Pour the boiling vinegar over the the beetroot, to cover it by 1.25 cm ($^1/_2$ inch). Gently tap the jars to remove any air pockets.

5 Seal the jars and label. Keep in a cool dark place for 3 weeks before using, to allow the flavours to develop.

Fills about three 300 ml (10 fl oz) jars

TANGY PICKLED MUSHROOMS

INGREDIENTS

675 g ($1^1/_2$ lb) mushrooms

7.5 cm (3 inch) piece of fresh
root ginger

1 lemon

1 onion

1 litre ($1^3/_4$ pints) white wine
vinegar

15 ml (1 tbsp) sea salt

5 ml (1 tsp) black
peppercorns

Although mushrooms make a great pickle, they do not keep as long as many other vegetables. Make small amounts, keeping them in the refrigerator, and eat them quickly.

1 Wipe the mushrooms with a damp cloth and trim the stalks so that they are even with the caps. Do not wash or peel them. Put the mushrooms into a saucepan.

2 Peel the root ginger with a small sharp knife, and cut it into quarters. Pare the zest from the lemon, with a vegetable peeler, and cut the zest into thin strips. Add the ginger and lemon strips to the mushrooms.

3 Peel and thinly slice the onion and add to the pan with all the remaining ingredients. Bring the mixture to a boil, and simmer for 15–20 minutes, or until the mushrooms are tender.

4 Lift the mushrooms out of the cooking liquid with a slotted spoon and pack into sterilized jars.

5 Strain the liquid, pour it back into the pan, and return to a boil. Pour it over the mushrooms, to cover them by 1.25 cm ($^1/_2$ inch).

6 Seal the jars, label, and keep in the refrigerator. The mushrooms are now ready to use.

Fills about three 300 ml (10 fl oz) jars

COOK'S TIP Use close-capped or tiny button mushrooms for this recipe. They should be completely fresh and pure white, with pale pink gills.

SWEET PICKLED BEANS

INGREDIENTS

675 g (1½ lb) green beans

15 ml (1 tbsp) Pickling Spice (see recipe, page 126)

15 ml (1 tbsp) black peppercorns

480 ml (16 fl oz) white wine vinegar

75 g (3 oz) sugar

1 bay leaf

1 garlic clove

1 onion

1 red pepper

4 large sprigs of dill

Serve pickled beans as an hors d'oeuvre or with egg mayonnaise.

1 Top and tail the beans and cut into 7.5 cm (3 inch) lengths. Put them into a pan of boiling water and boil for 1 minute. Drain, rinse under cold running water, and drain again.

2 Put the pickling spice and peppercorns on a square of muslin and tie up tightly into a bag with a long piece of string. Tie the bag to the handle of a saucepan. Put the vinegar, sugar, bay leaf, and garlic clove into the saucepan.

3 Stir the mixture over a low heat, with a wooden spoon, until the sugar has completely dissolved. Bring to a boil and simmer for 10 minutes. Remove and discard the muslin bag, bay leaf, and garlic clove. Leave to cool.

4 Meanwhile, peel and dice the onion. Core, seed, and dice the red pepper. Mix the two together and set aside.

5 Pack the beans upright into sterilized jars. Spoon in the onion and pepper mixture to within 2.5 cm (1 inch) of the tops. Add 2 sprigs of dill to each jar and pour in the sweetened vinegar to cover the beans by 1.25 cm (½ inch).

6 Seal the jars and label. Keep in a cool dark place for 2 weeks before using, to allow the flavours to develop.

Fills about two 600 ml (1 pint) jars

JAPANESE PICKLED GINGER

INGREDIENTS

225 g (8 oz) fresh root ginger

sea salt

240 ml (8 fl oz) rice vinegar

15 ml (1 tbsp) sugar

a few drops red food colouring

ORIENTAL PICKLE
Japanese Pickled Ginger, known as shoga or gari in Japan, has both a tart and a sweet taste.

In Japan, pickled ginger is always served with sushi – vinegared rice garnished with raw fish and shellfish. It also goes well with other seafoods and poultry. Traditionally, fresh plum juice is used to subtly colour the pickling liquid, but red food colouring works just as well.

1 Peel the ginger and cut it along the grain into the thinnest possible slivers. Put them into a bowl, cover with cold water, and leave to stand for 30 minutes.

2 Drain the ginger, and put it into a saucepan of boiling water. Bring back to a boil, drain again, and let cool. Return the ginger to the bowl and sprinkle lightly with salt.

3 In a saucepan, combine the vinegar and sugar. Stir over a low heat until the sugar has completely dissolved. Stir in a few drops of red food colouring. Pour the vinegar mixture over the ginger, making sure it is completely submerged. Cover the bowl and let the ginger stand in a cool dark place for 2 weeks before using, to allow the flavours to develop.

4 Transfer the ginger and liquid to a sterilized jar. Seal the jar, label, and keep in the refrigerator.

Fills one 350 ml (12 fl oz) jar

FIVE-SPICE PEACHES

*Bottle up the taste of summer with these juicy peaches. Spiced
and enveloped in a fragrant sweet and sour syrup,
they make an ideal partner for cold meats,
especially pork and ham. Pack them into one large jar,
or two smaller ones, for individual gifts.*

INGREDIENTS

1.8 kg (4 lb) peaches

600 ml (1 pint) white wine
vinegar

12 black peppercorns

5 ml (1 tsp) whole cloves

4 cardamom pods

2 cinnamon sticks

2 star anise

1 kg (2 lb) sugar

**Fills one 1.15 litre
(2 pint) jar**

1 ◄ Bring a saucepan of
water to a boil and put
each peach into it for
30–40 seconds. The
timing will depend
on the ripeness of
the fruit. Remove
the peaches
with a slotted
spoon and
transfer
to a
bowl
of iced water.
Leave to cool, then
drain and dry well.

PICKING PEACHES
*Select your peaches for pickling at
the height of the season when their
skins blush with a rosy bloom.*

2 ▲ Halve the peaches,
using the indentation
on one side as a cutting
guide. Stone and peel them.
Discard the stones and skin
and set the peaches aside.

3 ▶ Bring the wine vinegar and spices to a boil in a preserving pan. Add the sugar and stir, over a low heat, until it has completely dissolved.

4 ▼ Boil the mixture for 2 minutes. Add the peach halves and simmer for 4–5 minutes, or until the peaches are tender when pierced with a knife.

SPLENDID SPICES
Whole spices are used rather than ground ones to give the peaches a crystal-clear syrup in which to soak and mature.

FINISHING TOUCHES
Ladle the syrup right to the top of the jar so that the peaches are completely covered. If using more than one jar, make sure the spices are evenly divided between the jars so that all the peaches can share their flavour.

5 ▲ Transfer the peaches to a sterilized jar, to within 1.25 cm (¹/₂ inch) of the top. Boil the syrup for a further 2–3 minutes, until it has slightly reduced.

6 ▶ Pour syrup over the peaches. Seal the jar and label. Keep in a cool dark place for 2 months before using, to allow the flavours to develop.

CHUTNEYS

ORIGINALLY FROM INDIA, where their Hindu name, *chatni*, means "strongly spiced", chutneys are much more than that – rich concoctions of fruits, vegetables, herbs, and spices, that are slow-cooked with vinegar and sugar to create a sweet-sour condiment. The most popular spices are the aromatic ones – cinnamon, ginger, allspice, and cardamom. Mango chutney is surely the greatest favourite, and is a good way to preserve the perfumed flavour of mangoes with their all-too-short season.

Chutneys can be freshly made to eat right away, but the cooked version is the most commonly known. Cooked chutneys are an ideal side dish, and they go with almost anything – hot or cold meats and poultry, cheeses, vegetables, and eggs. They keep well, improving with age.

A chutney invites improvization. Although mango chutney is a classic, magnificent chutneys can be made with nectarines, peaches, pears, apricots, beetroots, green and red tomatoes, pineapples, papayas – the list is almost endless. They can be very hot, if made with chillies, or mild, with their sweetness predominating. The perfect time for chutney making is when there is a glut of fruits and vegetables on the market, and there is no reason why a gifted cook should not experiment with new combinations of ingredients – dates with oranges, green tomatoes with apples, and marrow with apricots are but a few of the possibilities.

MAKING CHUTNEYS

❧ Select the ingredients. Chutney is perfect for using up misshapen and bruised fruits and vegetables that are not suitable for other preserves in which appearance is important. The produce can also be riper than that used for jam making, but not over-ripe. Other ingredients added for flavour are spices, vinegar, dried fruits, nuts, and sugar. White sugar, or brown (for its colour and flavour) can be used, so too can honey, golden syrup, and molasses, but in small quantities only, as they can crystallize during storage.
❧ Wash the fruits and vegetables and, if necessary, peel or skin. Chop the fruits and vegetables by hand, or in a food processor for a finer, less chunky chutney.

❧ Long slow cooking is best for chutneys, so that the ingredients can break down and all the flavour be extracted. It may be necessary to simmer hard- or thick-skinned fruits or vegetables, such as unripe pears, carrots, or gooseberries, in vinegar first to soften them.
❧ The chutney is ready when it has reduced and thickened to a jam-like consistency. There should be no runny vinegar visible when a spoon is drawn in a line across the bottom of the pan. Spoon the chutney into warmed sterilized jars (see page 11), to within 3 mm ($^1/_8$ inch) of the tops, and stir with a metal skewer to remove any air pockets.

How to seal and store
Seal the jars very tightly with non-corrosive lids. Metal screw-top lids with plastic linings are the best choice, because they ensure that the vinegar does not evaporate and dry out the chutney. Label the jars. Although chutneys can be eaten immediately, most are best left for 1 month before eating, to allow the flavours to develop. Chutneys generally keep for up to 1 year if stored in a cool dry and dark place, but some chutneys have different storage times, which are given in individual recipes.

What can go wrong and why
If the chutney dries out or shrinks in the jar, it has been over-boiled, not covered tightly enough, or stored in a warm place. Mouldy chutney is caused by insufficient vinegar, under-cooking, or the use of unsterilized jars. Liquid on the surface of a chutney is a result of insufficient boiling down of the mixture.

DARK MANGO CHUTNEY

Some mango chutneys are sweet and light – this one is mysteriously dark and spicy. No individual flavour dominates, the ingredients just blend together in a simply delightful way.

INGREDIENTS

1.4 kg (3 lb) mangoes

30 ml (2 tbsp) salt

100 g (4 oz) tamarind pulp

75 g (3 oz) fresh root ginger

15 g (1/2 oz) dried red chillies

480 ml (16 fl oz) cider vinegar

675 g (1 1/2 lb) light soft brown sugar

100 g (4 oz) raisins

5 ml (1 tsp) ground allspice

Makes about 1.8 kg (4 lb)

1 ◀ Cut each mango on both sides of the stone; slice the flesh away from the stone and discard the stone. Peel the mango slices and cut the flesh into chunks. Put the mango flesh into a non-metallic bowl, stir in the salt, cover, and leave for 2 hours.

2 Put the tamarind pulp into a bowl and pour over boiling water to cover the pulp. Cover and leave for 1 hour, then drain off the excess water.

3 Put the tamarind pulp into a plastic sieve set over a bowl. Press the pulp through the sieve; discard the seeds. Drain the mangoes. Rinse the mango chunks in a plastic sieve under cold running water, until all the salt is washed off. Drain well. Put the sieved tamarind pulp and the mango flesh into a preserving pan.

4 Peel and finely chop the ginger. Halve the chillies lengthwise; remove and discard all the seeds. Either tear the chillies into small pieces with your fingers, or chop them with a small knife.

MYSTERY MANGO
A delicious complement to curries, simple cheese platters, and hot or cold meats.

5 ◀ Stir the ginger, chillies, vinegar, sugar, raisins, and allspice into the mango and tamarind mixture. Bring to a boil, stirring. Simmer over a medium heat, stirring, for 30 minutes, or until the mangoes are tender and the chutney has reduced and thickened.

6 ▶ Test by pulling the back of the spoon across the bottom of the pan. There should be no runny vinegar visible.

7 Spoon the chutney into warmed sterilized jars, to within 3 mm (1/8 inch) of the tops. Stir, if necessary, to remove any air pockets. Seal the jars and label. The chutney is now ready to use.

RED TOMATO CHUTNEY

A mild and aromatic fruit and vegetable chutney that is made with a careful balance of spices. Let the flavours blend and mature by storing the chutney for a couple of months before eating. It is the perfect accompaniment to thick wedges of mature cheese and crusty fresh bread.

INGREDIENTS

1.4 kg (3 lb) ripe tomatoes

675 g (1¹/₂ lb) small onions

1 kg (2 lb) cooking apples

480 ml (16 fl oz) white wine vinegar

350 g (12 oz) sugar

175 g (6 oz) sultanas

10 ml (2 tsp) salt

5 ml (1 tsp) ground cloves

5 ml (1 tsp) ground ginger

2.5 ml (¹/₂ tsp) cayenne pepper

Makes about 2 kg (4¹/₂ lb)

1 ◄ Cut the cores out of the tomatoes. Put the tomatoes into a bowl and cover with boiling water. Leave for 15–20 seconds, or until the skins start to split. Transfer the tomatoes to a bowl of cold water. Remove from the water one at a time and peel away the skins, using a sharp knife. Roughly chop the tomatoes.

2 ► Peel and thinly slice the onions. Peel, core, and chop the apples. Put the tomatoes, onions, and apples into a preserving pan. Add all the remaining ingredients and stir to combine.

3 ◄ Bring to a boil, stirring. Lower the heat and simmer, stirring often, for 40–45 minutes, or until the fruit and vegetables are soft and the chutney has reduced and thickened. Test by drawing the back of the spoon across the bottom of the pan. There should be no runny liquid visible.

4 Spoon the chutney into warmed sterilized jars, to within 3 mm (¹/₈ inch) of the tops. Stir to remove any air pockets. Seal the jars and label. Keep in a cool dark place for 2 months before using, to allow the flavours to develop.

LEMON AND MUSTARD SEED CHUTNEY

INGREDIENTS

8 large lemons, total weight
about 1.8 kg (4 lb)

450 g (1 lb) onions

50 g (2 oz) salt

450 ml (15 fl oz) water

1 kg (2 lb) sugar

225 g (8 oz) sultanas

25 g (1 oz) mustard seeds

10 ml (2 tsp) ground ginger

5 ml (1 tsp) cayenne pepper

900 ml (1½ pints) cider
vinegar

An excellent accompaniment for a Cheddar cheese ploughman's platter. If the mustard seeds are omitted, the plain lemon chutney tastes good with Thai or Indian food.

1 Cut the lemons into 3 mm (⅛ inch) slices. Cut the slices into quarters; remove and discard any pips. Peel and slice the onions.

2 Layer the lemon and onion slices with the salt in a large non-metallic bowl. Put a plate on top to keep the mixture lightly pressed down. Leave, covered, for 24 hours, to draw out the excess moisture.

3 Rinse the lemon and onion slices in a plastic sieve or colander under cold running water until all the salt is washed off. Put them into a preserving pan and pour in water to cover. Bring to a boil. Simmer over a low heat, stirring occasionally, for 35 minutes, or until the lemon peel is very tender.

4 Add the remaining ingredients and return to a boil, stirring. Simmer over a low heat, stirring occasionally, for 45–50 minutes, or until the chutney has reduced and thickened.

5 Spoon the chutney into warmed sterilized jars, to within 3 mm (⅛ inch) of the tops. Seal the jars and label. Keep in a cool dark place for 2 months before using, to allow the flavours to develop.

Makes about 2.25 kg (5 lb)

PRUNE AND HAZELNUT CHUTNEY

INGREDIENTS

1 kg (2 lb) prunes

675 g (1½ lb) cooking apples

60 ml (4 tbsp) water

575 g (1¼ lb) dark soft
brown sugar

225 g (8 oz) hazelnuts

600 ml (1 pint) red wine
vinegar

5 ml (1 tsp) curry powder

5 ml (1 tsp) ground cinnamon

2.5 ml (½ tsp) ground
allspice

1.25 ml (¼ tsp) cayenne
pepper

This fruity chutney does not need a long time to mature, in fact, it seems to have a better flavour when it is young. Serve with chicken or ham.

1 Put the prunes into a bowl and cover with boiling water. Leave to stand for 24 hours.

2 Peel, core, and finely chop the apples. Put them into a preserving pan with the water and 50 g (2 oz) of the sugar. Stir over a low heat until the sugar has completely dissolved. Simmer for 10 minutes, or until the apples are tender.

3 Chop the nuts finely. Drain the prunes and remove their stones. Chop the prunes and add to the pan with the nuts and all the remaining ingredients. Stir to combine.

4 Bring to a boil, stirring. Simmer over a low heat, stirring frequently, for 30 minutes, or until the chutney has reduced and thickened.

5 Spoon the chutney into warmed sterilized jars, to within 3 mm (⅛ inch) of the tops. Seal the jars and label. Keep in a cool dark place for 6 weeks before using, to allow the flavours to develop.

Makes about 2.25 kg (5 lb)

Banana Chutney

INGREDIENTS

450 g (1 lb) bananas

225 g (8 oz) dried dates

50 g (2 oz) crystallized ginger

450 ml (15 fl oz) white wine
vinegar

finely grated zest and juice of
1 lemon and 1 orange

225 g (8 oz) raisins

275 g (10 oz) dark soft brown
sugar

10 ml (2 tsp) each of salt and
curry powder

1 Peel the bananas and cut the flesh into small pieces. Stone and chop the dates, and chop the crystallized ginger.

2 Put all the prepared ingredients into a preserving pan with the vinegar, lemon and orange zest and juice, and bring to a boil. Lower the heat and simmer, stirring occasionally with a wooden spoon, for 30 minutes.

3 Add all the remaining ingredients and stir over a low heat until the sugar has completely dissolved. Return to a boil and simmer, stirring frequently, for a further 10–15 minutes, or until the chutney has reduced and thickened.

4 Spoon the chutney into warmed sterilized jars, to within 3 mm (1/8 inch) of the tops. Seal the jars and label. Keep in a cool dark place for 1–2 months before using, to allow the flavours to develop.

Makes about 1.15 kg (2 1/2 lb)

Papaya Chutney

INGREDIENTS

1 kg (2 lb) unripe papaya

100 g (4 oz) cashew nuts

50 g (2 oz) fresh root ginger

3 large garlic cloves

2 fresh hot red chillies

225 g (8 oz) sultanas

450 g (1 lb) light soft brown
sugar

480 ml (16 fl oz) cider
vinegar

10 ml (2 tsp) salt

1 Peel the papaya, scrape out and discard the black seeds, and cut the flesh into 2.5 cm (1 inch) cubes.

2 Toast the cashew nuts on a baking sheet in a 180°C (350°F, Gas 4) oven until lightly browned. Let them cool slightly, and coarsely chop. Peel and finely chop the root ginger and garlic cloves. Halve, seed, and chop the chillies.

3 Put all the ingredients into a preserving pan. Simmer, stirring occasionally, for 30 minutes, or until the chutney has reduced and thickened.

4 Spoon the chutney into warmed sterilized jars, to within 3 mm (1/8 inch) of the tops. Seal the jars and label. Keep in a cool dark place. The chutney can be used immediately, but it improves if stored for 2 weeks before using, to allow the flavours to develop.

Makes about 1.25 kg (2 3/4 lb)

Orange Chutney

INGREDIENTS

6 oranges, total weight about
1 kg (2 lb)

225 g (8 oz) onions

450 g (1 lb) fresh dates

600 ml (1 pint) white wine
vinegar

10 ml (2 tsp) each of ground
ginger and coriander

1 Peel the oranges, discarding the peel and pips. Chop the flesh, and put it, with any juice, into a preserving pan.

2 Peel and chop the onions, and stone and chop the dates. Add to the pan with the oranges. Add all the remaining ingredients and bring to a boil. Simmer, stirring occasionally, for 1 hour, or until the chutney has reduced and thickened.

3 Spoon into warmed sterilized jars, to within 3 mm (1/8 inch) of the tops. Seal the jars and label. Keep in a cool dark place for 1 1/2–2 months before using, to allow the flavours to develop.

Makes about 1.1 kg (2 1/4 lb)

Beetroot Chutney

INGREDIENTS

2 cooking apples

1 onion

240 ml (8 fl oz) malt vinegar

10 ml (2 tsp) freshly grated
root ginger

5 ml (1 tsp) ground allspice

2 whole cloves

450 g (1 lb) cooked beetroots
(see box, right)

50 g (2 oz) dark muscovado
sugar

50 g (2 oz) raisins

1 Core and slice the apples. Peel and slice the onion. Put the apples and onion into a preserving pan. Add the vinegar with the root ginger, allspice, and cloves; bring to a boil. Simmer, stirring occasionally, for 20 minutes.

2 Peel the cooked beetroots, finely chop them, and add to the pan with the sugar and raisins. Bring to a boil and simmer for 15 minutes.

3 Spoon the chutney into warmed sterilized jars, to within 3 mm ($^1/_8$ inch) of the tops. Seal the jars and label. The chutney is now ready to use.

Makes about 1 kg (2 lb)

To Cook Beetroots Do not peel them before cooking because they will "bleed". Bring a pan of salted water to a boil, add beetroots, and simmer for 20–30 minutes. Drain and cool.

Bengal Chutney

INGREDIENTS

225 g (8 oz) carrots

1 onion

450 g (1 lb) cooking apples

100 g (4 oz) raisins

100 g (4 oz) freshly grated
horseradish

225 g (8 oz) demerara sugar

10 ml (2 tsp) salt

15 ml (1 tbsp) ground ginger

15 ml (1 tbsp) curry powder

5 ml (1 tsp) mustard seeds

30 ml (2 tbsp) golden syrup

300 ml (10 fl oz) vinegar

Chutneys are served as condiments in an Indian meal in the same way as salt and pepper are in the West. This chutney comes from Bengal, in northern India.

1 Peel and slice the carrots and onion. Peel, core, and slice the apples. Put all the sliced ingredients into a saucepan.

2 Add all the remaining ingredients to the pan. Simmer, stirring occasionally, for 50 minutes, or until the chutney has reduced and thickened.

3 Spoon the chutney into warmed sterilized jars, to within 3 mm ($^1/_8$ inch) of the tops. Seal the jars and label. Keep in a cool dark place for 6 weeks before using, to allow the flavours to develop.

**Makes about
1.15 kg (2¹/2 lb)**

LUXURIOUS OILS & VINEGARS

FLAVOURED OILS

INFUSING OILS with a single flavour or a compatible combination of herbs and spices is a lovely way to make personalized gifts for friends. Almost any herb or spice can be used, along with aromatic fruits, such as oranges, lemons, or limes. Flowering herbs, such as rosemary and thyme, added to the finished bottles create a pretty effect.

Today's cooks have a wide choice of oils to work from, each with a special flavour of its own. Everyday oils – corn, rapeseed (canola), safflower, and sunflower – are guaranteed not to dominate the taste of the ingredients with which they are combined; these oils are generally suitable for infusing with the more pungent herbs and spices. Luxury oils, including walnut and hazelnut, and the exotics, such as mustard oil used in Indian cooking, and the bright orange, nutty palm oil used in Brazilian cooking – already have their own distinctive tastes and are not usually chosen for making flavoured oils. The greatest of all the oils for flavouring is olive, and the best quality is extra-virgin olive oil, made from the first cold pressing of the finest olives.

Flavoured oils can be used in marinades, salad dressings, or for the initial sauté in a stir-fry; in fact, for any dish in which you would use an ordinary oil. Simply ensure that the taste of the oil complements the ingredients you are using.

MAKING FLAVOURED OILS

❧ Start by sterilizing glass bottles (see page 11). It is best to choose a small size, because oils can turn rancid after opening and small amounts will be used more quickly.
❧ Select your flavourings. If you are using herbs, they should be freshly picked and lightly dried on kitchen paper to remove excess moisture, then bruised lightly to release their aroma immediately. Dried spices, such as cinnamon sticks, peppercorns, and chillies, should be as fresh as possible so that their maximum flavour is extracted. Fresh garlic cloves lend pungency, but should only be used in small amounts. If garlic is added to flavour the oil, it is important to keep the oil refrigerated and to use it within 2 weeks.
❧ Insert the prepared flavourings into the bottles, then pour in the oil to fill and cover all the ingredients (so mould cannot grow). Seal the bottles.
❧ Leave for about 2 weeks in a cool dark place. During this time the flavour will develop in the oil, so taste it occasionally to see when it is ready to use. Shake the bottle a few times, especially if it contains ingredients such as paprika that settle on the bottom. If you prefer the flavour not to get any stronger at this stage, or if you want

the oil to last longer (particularly if it contains fresh ingredients), strain it through a double layer of muslin into freshly sterilized bottles. For decoration and easy identification, a fresh herb sprig can be added to herb oils, or a twist of orange or lemon zest to citrus oils.

How to seal and store
Seal tightly in bottles with non-corrosive, screw-top lids, label, then keep in the refrigerator for 3–6 months. The storage time will depend on the flavouring of the oil. Those that contain fresh ingredients, such as herbs or fruits, unless strained first, will only last about 3 months. Oils that have been infused with dried ingredients will last about 6 months.

What can go wrong and why
A flavoured oil will become cloudy if its flavouring, such as fresh onion, contains too much water. If this happens, use up the oil as soon as possible, because it can quickly become rancid. Other reasons for an oil turning rancid are incorrect storage, faulty sealing of bottles, and the oil coming into contact with direct sunlight and heat.

FIERY CHILLI OIL

Brilliant red chillies, infused in warm oil, produce a glowing colour and potent taste that can be diluted by using fewer chillies than suggested here, or by taking out the chilli seeds. Use chilli oil to sauté onions and garlic for stir-fries, sauces, casseroles, or soups, or mix it with vinegar to make a salad dressing. It will give every dish an instant burst of flavour.

INGREDIENTS

12 dried red chillies

480 ml (16 fl oz) rapeseed (canola) oil or corn oil

22.5 ml (1¹/₂ tbsp) cayenne pepper

30 ml (2 tbsp) roasted sesame oil

Makes about 480 ml (16 fl oz)

1 ◀ Finely chop the chillies. Put them into a medium saucepan and pour in the rapeseed or corn oil. Simmer over a very low heat for 10 minutes. (Don't let the oil get too hot; over-heating will spoil its keeping qualities). Remove from the heat and leave to cool.

2 ◀ Stir in the cayenne pepper and the sesame oil. Cover the pan and leave for 12 hours, to allow the flavours to develop.

IDENTIFICATION PARADE
Two or three dried chillies added to the bottle of oil will make it readily identifiable on the kitchen shelf.

3 ▶ Line a funnel with a double layer of muslin and strain the flavoured oil through it into a sterilized bottle, to within 3 mm (¹/₈ inch) of the top.

4 If you like, add 2–3 whole dried red chillies to the bottle of oil. Seal the bottle and label. The oil is now ready to use.

COOK'S TIP When chillies are lightly cooked in oil, their flavour is released instantly, so the oil can be used right away rather than left for 1–2 weeks.

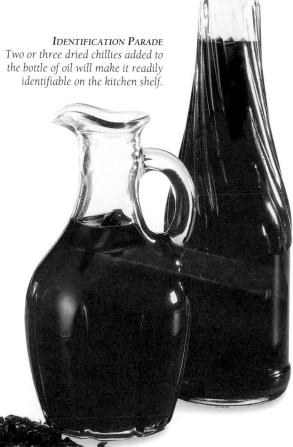

ANNATTO OIL

INGREDIENTS

50 g (2 oz) annatto seeds

240 ml (8 fl oz) rapeseed (canola) oil or corn oil

This oil, known in Spanish as aceite de achiote, can be used to sauté fish, shellfish, poultry, and vegetables.

1 Put the annatto seeds and oil into a small heavy-based saucepan. Simmer over a low heat, stirring occasionally, for 1–5 minutes, or until the mixture turns a rich orange as the seeds give up their colour. The time needed depends on the freshness of the seeds. As soon as the colour of the oil begins to lighten from orange to gold, remove the pan from the heat and leave to cool.

2 Line a funnel with a double layer of muslin and strain the flavoured oil through it into a sterilized bottle, to within 3 mm ($^1/_8$ inch) of the top.

3 Seal the bottle and label.

Makes about 240 ml (8 fl oz)

DID YOU KNOW?
Tiny triangular annatto seeds come from the flowering annatto tree, which grows in the Caribbean, and in Central and South America. The seeds turn oil a golden colour, and give a subtle spicy flavour.

SWEET PAPRIKA OIL

INGREDIENTS

60 ml (4 tbsp) sweet paprika

1 litre (1$^3/_4$ pints) extra-virgin olive oil

DO-IT-YOURSELF FUNNEL
A handmade funnel is useful for spooning ground spices into bottles. Make it with paper or foil.

1 Divide the paprika equally between sterilized bottles: spoon it through a handmade paper funnel placed in the neck of each of the bottles.

2 Pour the extra-virgin olive oil into the bottles, to within 3 mm ($^1/_8$ inch) of the tops.

3 Seal the bottles and shake well. Keep in a cool dark place for 1 week before using, to allow the flavours to develop. Shake the bottles from time to time.

4 Line a funnel with a double layer of muslin and strain the flavoured oil through it into freshly sterilized bottles. Seal the bottles and label. The oil is now ready to use.

Makes about 1 litre (1$^3/_4$ pints)

ORANGE AND CORIANDER OIL

INGREDIENTS

30 ml (2 tbsp) coriander seeds

4 strips of dried orange zest (see box, right)

1 litre (1$^3/_4$ pints) extra-virgin olive oil

1 Lightly crush the coriander seeds in a mortar and pestle, being careful not to break them up completely. Alternatively, use the end of a rolling pin to crush them. Divide the coriander seeds equally between sterilized bottles.

2 If necessary, cut the dried orange zest to a size that will fit through the necks of the bottles. Add the zest to the coriander. Pour in the oil, to within 3 mm ($^1/_8$ inch) of the tops.

3 Seal the bottles and shake well. Label and keep in a cool dark place for 1 week before using, to allow the flavours to develop. Shake the bottles from time to time.

Makes about 1 litre (1$^3/_4$ pints)

COOK'S TIP
To dry orange zest: preheat the oven on its lowest setting. Peel wide strips of zest from top to bottom of an orange. Put the strips on a baking sheet and leave in the oven for 1$^1/_4$ hours, or until dry.

Mixed Herb Oil

Ingredients

2 sprigs of fresh rosemary

2 sprigs of fresh thyme

2 pickling onions

2 bay leaves

12 black peppercorns

1 litre (1 3/4 pints) extra-virgin
olive oil

1 Lightly bruise the rosemary and thyme to release their flavours. Peel and finely slice the pickling onions.

2 Divide the bruised herbs, onion slices, bay leaves, and peppercorns equally between 2 sterilized bottles.

3 Pour in the oil, to within 3 mm (1/8 inch) of the tops, making sure that the ingredients are completely covered.

4 Seal the bottles and shake well. Label and keep in a cool dark place for 2 weeks before using, to allow the flavours to develop. Shake the bottles from time to time.

Makes about 1 litre (1 3/4 pints)

Perfumed Thai Oil

Ingredients

4–6 sprigs of fresh coriander

6 pieces of fresh lemon grass

4 dried red chillies

1 litre (1 3/4 pints) rapeseed
(canola) oil or corn oil

1 Lightly bruise the coriander and lemon grass with the flat side of a chef's knife, to release their flavours.

2 Divide the bruised coriander and lemon grass, and the chillies, equally between sterilized bottles. Pour in the oil, to within 3 mm (1/8 inch) of tops.

3 Seal the bottles and shake well. Label and keep in a cool dark place for 2 weeks before using, to allow the flavours to develop. Remove the coriander and lemon grass after 2 weeks.

Makes about 1 litre (1 3/4 pints)

Indian Spice Oil

Ingredients

5 ml (1 tsp) Aromatic Garam
Masala (see recipe, page 125)

2.5 ml (1/2 tsp) garlic powder

2.5 ml (1/2 tsp) ground
coriander

2.5 ml (1/2 tsp) ground cumin

2.5 ml (1/2 tsp) chilli powder

2.5 ml (1/2 tsp) ground
turmeric

10 ml (2 tsp) dried fenugreek
leaves

2 whole cloves

1 litre (1 3/4 pints) rapeseed
(canola) oil or corn oil

This powerfully flavoured oil adds a tang to marinated or sautéed food, and is also ideal for barbecued steak and chicken.

1 Put all the powdered spices into a small bowl and mix well together. Divide the spice mixture equally between 2 sterilized bottles by spooning them through a funnel placed in each bottle neck. Divide the fenugreek leaves and cloves between the bottles.

2 Pour in the oil, to within 3 mm (1/8 inch) of the tops. Seal the bottles and shake well. Keep in a cool dark place for 1–2 weeks before using, to allow the flavours to develop. Shake the bottles from time to time.

3 Line a funnel with a double layer of muslin and strain the oil through it into 2 freshly sterilized bottles. Seal the bottles and label. The oil is now ready to use.

Makes about 1 litre (1 3/4 pints)

From left to right, *Perfumed Thai Oil, Sweet Paprika Oil, and Mixed Herb Oil*

OIL OF ITALY

INGREDIENTS

4 fresh sage leaves

4–6 sprigs of fresh basil

12 black peppercorns

1 litre (1 3/4 pints) extra-virgin olive oil

Italian cooks adore the earthy taste of sage and the semi-sweet flavour of basil, both of which are combined in this oil. Use it for tossing with pasta, or for drizzling over a mozzarella cheese and tomato salad.

1 Lightly bruise the sage and basil to release their flavours. Divide the bruised herbs and the peppercorns equally between sterilized bottles. Pour in the olive oil, to within 3 mm (1/8 inch) of the tops of the bottles.

2 Seal the bottles and shake well. Label and keep in a cool dark place for 2 weeks before using, to allow the flavours to develop. Shake the bottles from time to time.

Makes about 1 litre (1 3/4 pints)

PROVENÇAL OIL

INGREDIENTS

25 g (1 oz) mixed fresh herbs and spices, e.g. fennel stalks, oregano, tarragon, thyme, rosemary, coriander seeds, 1 bay leaf, and 1 dried red chilli

600 ml (1 pint) extra-virgin olive oil

An intriguing mix of herbs and spices goes into this oil, which takes on the scent of southern France as it soaks up their flavours. The herbs and spices listed here are just one suggestion, but you can experiment with other combinations.

1 Put the herbs and spices into a sterilized bottle. Pour in the olive oil, to within 3 mm (1/8 inch) of the top, making sure that the herbs are completely covered.

2 Seal the bottle and shake well. Label and keep in a cool dark place for 2 weeks before using, to allow the flavours to develop. Shake the bottle from time to time.

Makes about 600 ml (1 pint)

ROSEMARY OIL

INGREDIENTS

4–6 large sprigs of fresh rosemary

1 litre (1 3/4 pints) extra-virgin olive oil

This is the simplest of flavoured oils. Any other single herb can be used to flavour oil in the same way: lemon balm, tarragon, marjoram, oregano, mint, or thyme. For a stronger flavour, add extra herb sprigs and keep for longer before opening.

1 Lightly bruise the rosemary sprigs (see box, below), to release their flavour.

2 Divide the sprigs of rosemary equally between sterilized bottles. Pour in the olive oil, to within 3 mm (1/8 inch) of the tops, making sure the rosemary is completely covered.

3 Seal the bottles and shake well. Label and keep in a cool dark place for 2 weeks before using, to allow the flavours to develop. Shake the bottles from time to time.

Makes about 1 litre (1 3/4 pints)

DID YOU KNOW? To extract the full flavour from fresh herbs, it is best to bruise them just before using. Put the herbs on a chopping board and lay a large chef's knife on top of them. Using the palm of your hand, press down firmly on the flat of the knife.

PRESERVES IN OIL

OLIVE OIL, richly aromatic and fruity, is wonderful as a preserver of foods. In the commercial world, artichoke hearts, anchovies, sardines, and tuna are all traditionally preserved in olive oil. We may take them for granted, yet those of us addicted to the sharp, salty flavour of anchovies in a Caesar salad, or chunks of tuna tossed in a *salade Niçoise*, would greatly miss these treats if there were no oil to preserve them for us.

There are many gifts to be made at home, using a variety of foods with oil as a preservative. Olives, mushrooms, feta and goat's cheeses, and lemons, will all be transformed once bathed and soaked in oil. Pack them in your favourite jars, jazz them up with fresh herbs and spices to bring out their flavours, top up with oil, and you will have luxurious delicacies for serving with salads, as appetizers, or as accompaniments. Sun-dried tomatoes also gain extra flavour when they are stored in oil. The concentrated tomato taste will soon brighten up the topping on a pizza, the filling in a quiche, or a sauce over pasta. There is an added advantage to be gained from this process. At the same time as being kept fresh by the oil, the preserved ingredients impart their delicious flavour to it. So, once they have been eaten, the flavoured oil can be used for cooking and in salad dressings.

PRESERVES IN OIL

❦ Select the oil. The choice will depend upon how strong you want the flavour to be. Ordinary olive oil is much milder in flavour than extra-virgin olive oil. Corn oil or sunflower oil can be used if a neutrally flavoured oil is required. Nut oils are not a good choice, because they tend to go rancid much more quickly than other oils.

❦ Choose the ingredients. Vegetables can be preserved in oil, but use only those which can be processed in some way first to remove their excess water. The most usual methods are salting, such as with salt-cured olives and lemons, and drying, for vegetables like mushrooms and tomatoes. Mushrooms can also be cooked to extract their moisture. Feta and goat's cheeses take well to being preserved in olive oil and, after the cheese has been eaten, you can use the cheesy-flavoured oil for cooking or in salad dressings. Once you have chosen which foods to preserve, marry them with some scented herb sprigs or pungent spices, to enhance their natural flavours.

❦ Pack the chosen ingredients and any seasonings into dry sterilized jars (see page 11), then pour in the oil to almost fill the jars and completely cover the ingredients.

❦ Leave for about 1 week in a cool dark place, so that the oil can preserve and flavour the ingredients, and the ingredients flavour the oil. The longer you leave them, the more potent the taste.

How to seal and store
Seal tightly in jars with non-corrosive, screw-top lids. Choose a cool dark place for storage, or store in the refrigerator. Foods preserved in oil will then keep for up to 3 months. Any foods preserved in oil that contain garlic should always be stored in the refrigerator, and used within 1–2 weeks. You must make sure that the contents of all jars are always well covered with oil.

What can go wrong and why
If the oil goes rancid quickly, the jars have been stored in direct sunlight, which also destroys the vitamins in the oil. The oil may also go rancid if an opened bottle of oil is used for preserving the foods. Always break the seal on a brand new bottle of oil, so that you know it is fresh. If the contents of the jars start to go mouldy, it could be because they are not completely covered with oil.

GREEK OLIVES IN OIL

Olive oil, with its earthy aroma and flavour, is the most perfect complement to the grand and succulent Kalamata olive. It has a dual role in this recipe – to preserve the olives and absorb their flavour – so that once you have eaten the oil-soaked olives, you can use the scented oil for cooking.

INGREDIENTS

675 g (1½ lb) black Kalamata olives, in brine

5 ml (1 tsp) coriander seeds

1 large sprig of fresh rosemary

300–350 ml (10–12 fl oz) extra-virgin olive oil

Fills one 1 litre (1¾ pint) jar

1 Drain the olives into a sieve and rinse them well under cold running water. Drain again and dry the olives thoroughly on kitchen paper.

2 ◄ Put the coriander seeds in a mortar and pestle and lightly crush them, being careful not to break them up completely. Alternatively, use the end of a rolling pin to break up the seeds.

3 ► Pack the olives into a sterilized jar, to within 2 cm (¾ inch) of the top, sprinkling with the coriander as you go. Tuck the sprig of rosemary down one side of the jar.

4 ▲ Pour in the olive oil almost to the top of the jar, making sure all the olives are covered by 1.25 cm (½ inch) oil. Use a metal skewer to push out any air pockets.

5 Seal the jar and label. Keep in a cool dark place for at least 1 week before using, to allow the flavours to develop.

RED-HOT LEMON SLICES IN OLIVE OIL

INGREDIENTS

6 lemons, total weight about 675 g (1 1/2 lb)

100 g (4 oz) sea salt

2 dried red chillies

2 dried bay leaves

25 ml (5 tsp) paprika

5 ml (1 tsp) chilli powder

300 ml (10 fl oz) extra-virgin olive oil

1 Cut the lemons evenly into slices about 5 mm ($\frac{1}{4}$ inch) thick. Remove all the pips from the slices.

2 Put the lemon slices in a single layer in a shallow non-metallic dish. Sprinkle the slices with the salt, and leave to stand, covered, for 24 hours to draw out the excess moisture.

3 Drain the lemon slices, leaving the salt on the surface. Roughly chop the chillies and crumble the bay leaves into small pieces. Mix them in a small bowl with the paprika and chilli powder.

4 Carefully pack the salt-encrusted lemon slices in neat layers into sterilized jars, to within 2 cm ($\frac{3}{4}$ inch) of the tops, sprinkling the spice mixture evenly between the layers as you go.

5 Pour in the oil almost to the tops of the jars, making sure the lemons are covered by 1.25 cm ($\frac{1}{2}$ inch). Seal the jars and label. Keep in a cool dark place for at least 1 week before using, to allow the flavours to develop.

Fills about two 480 ml (16 fl oz) jars

SUN-DRIED TOMATOES IN OLIVE OIL

INGREDIENTS

50 g (2 oz) sun-dried tomatoes

2 bay leaves

200 ml (7 fl oz) extra-virgin olive oil

1 Put the sun-dried tomatoes into a bowl and cover with boiling water. Leave for 5 minutes, then drain well in a plastic sieve and pat dry on kitchen paper.

2 Pack the tomatoes into sterilized jars, to within 2 cm ($\frac{3}{4}$ inch) of the tops, tucking in the bay leaves as you go. Pour in the oil almost to the tops of the jars, making sure the tomatoes are covered by 1.25 cm ($\frac{1}{2}$ inch).

3 Seal the jars and label. Keep in a cool dark place for at least 2 weeks before using, to allow the flavours to develop.

Fills about two 175 ml (6 fl oz) jars

MUSHROOMS IN OLIVE OIL

INGREDIENTS

675 g (1 1/2 lb) button mushrooms

480 ml (16 fl oz) extra-virgin olive oil

juice of 4 lemons

12 black peppercorns

4 peeled garlic cloves

2 bay leaves

1 Trim the mushroom stalks so that they are even with the caps. Put the mushrooms into a bowl. Add half of the oil, and stir in the remaining ingredients. Leave to stand for 3–4 hours.

2 Pour the mushroom mixture into a saucepan and bring to a boil. Simmer, stirring occasionally, for 15 minutes. Remove from the heat and leave to cool.

3 Drain the mushrooms in a plastic sieve and pat dry on kitchen paper. Pack them into a sterilized jar, to within 2 cm ($\frac{3}{4}$ inch) of the top. Pour in the remaining oil almost to the top of the jar, making sure the mushrooms are covered by 1.25 cm ($\frac{1}{2}$ inch). Seal the jar and label. Refrigerate and use within 2 weeks.

Fills one 1 litre (1 3/4 pint) jar

COOK'S TIP
Choose firm but moist mushrooms with no damp patches for this recipe, and wipe them clean with a damp tea-towel before using.

GOAT'S CHEESE WITH HERBS IN OIL

INGREDIENTS

*2 small round goat's cheeses
(crottins de Chavignol),
each weighing about 75 g (3 oz)*

3 sprigs of fresh thyme

3 bay leaves

6 black peppercorns

*240 ml (8 fl oz) extra-virgin
olive oil*

Leaving the cheese for 2–3 weeks ensures that the oil takes on the full flavour of the cheese and vice versa. Use the cheese in salads or on crisp French bread, and the oil for cooking.

1 Cut each goat's cheese into quarters. Pack the pieces into a sterilized jar, layering the cheese with the herbs and peppercorns as you go.

2 Pour in the olive oil to cover the cheese by 1.25 cm ($\frac{1}{2}$ inch).

3 Seal the jar and label. Keep in a cool dark place for 2–3 weeks before using, to allow the flavours to develop.

Fills one 350 ml (12 fl oz) jar

PROVENÇAL OLIVES IN AROMATIC OIL

INGREDIENTS

*675 g ($1\frac{1}{2}$ lb) green tanche
olives, in brine*

5 ml (1 tsp) fennel seeds

4 sprigs of fresh thyme

3 bay leaves

*about 350 ml (12 fl oz)
extra-virgin olive oil*

1 Drain the olives in a sieve and rinse them well under cold running water to remove any brine. Dry them on kitchen paper.

2 Pack the olives into a sterilized jar, sprinkling with the fennel seeds and tucking in the thyme and bay leaves as you go.

3 Pour in the olive oil to cover the olives by 1.25 cm ($\frac{1}{2}$ inch). Use a metal skewer to push out any air pockets, taking care not to pierce the olives.

4 Seal the jar and label. Keep in a cool dark place for 1–2 weeks before using, to allow the flavours to develop.

Fills one 1.15 litre (2 pint) jar

DID YOU KNOW?
Tanche olives are from Provence, in the south of France. If they are difficult to obtain, experiment with other green or black varieties.

FETA CHEESE WITH ROSEMARY IN OLIVE OIL

INGREDIENTS

175 g (6 oz) feta cheese

4–6 sprigs of fresh rosemary

12 black peppercorns

12 black olives

*240 ml (8 fl oz)
extra-virgin olive oil*

1 Drain the cheese and dry well on kitchen paper. Cut the cheese into 2 cm ($\frac{3}{4}$ inch) cubes.

2 Pack the cheese cubes into sterilized jars, to within 2 cm ($\frac{3}{4}$ inch) of the tops, tucking in the rosemary, peppercorns, and olives as you go.

3 Pour in the olive oil to cover the cheese by 1.25 cm ($\frac{1}{2}$ inch).

4 Seal the jars and label. Keep in a cool dark place for at least 1 week before using, to allow the flavours to develop.

Fills about two 240 ml (8 fl oz) jars

GREEK TREAT
Serve Feta Cheese with Rosemary in Olive Oil as a light lunch dish with warm continental breads.

FLAVOURED VINEGARS

COOKS WORLDWIDE have always welcomed vinegar into their kitchens, and have created endless roles for it to play. Through the art of pickling, it is a great preserver of nature's bounty, as well as a main ingredient for tenderizing tough meats, or making vinaigrette dressings for salads and crudités.

There are many basic types, from delicate Japanese rice vinegar through sharp wine vinegars to very robust malts, and exotic *aceto balsamico*. But add a variety of seasonings to flavour and colour vinegars, and they take on a whole new guise. Herbs, fruits, and spices – all of these can be steeped in vinegar. A dash of almost any sauce that has the blessing of a flavoured vinegar will banish blandness and add piquancy to soups, chowder, stews, and casseroles. Alternatively, use the vinegars combined with other seasonings to make marinades for meat, poultry, and seafood.

MAKING FLAVOURED VINEGARS

❧ Sterilize the bottles (see page 11). Plain uncoloured glass bottles are the best choice to show off the colour and flavourings of the vinegar. Dry the bottles thoroughly before using.

❧ Choose a good-quality vinegar with an acetic acid content of 5% or more. Malt vinegar can be used to make pickling vinegar for pickles, but choose wine, sherry, or cider vinegar to make flavoured vinegars for use in salad dressings and for cooking.

❧ Select the flavourings. For herb vinegars, use fresh herbs, preferably picked before they flower. Use a single herb or several, mixing pungent and delicate ones together to balance the flavours. Fruit vinegars are usually made from soft fruits, such as raspberries, blueberries, or blackberries, or from citrus fruits. Other flavourings include garlic, dried chillies, and spices.

❧ Wash and dry the flavourings, as necessary. The herbs, fruits, and spices may be lightly crushed to release flavour.

❧ Insert the flavourings into the bottles, and add the vinegar almost to the tops.

❧ After sealing the bottles, the vinegar is left for 2 weeks before using, to allow the flavours to develop (unless the mixture is lightly cooked first, in which case the vinegar can be used immediately).

❧ Straining the vinegar after its initial storage ensures that it lasts longer and becomes more clear. You may need to strain the vinegar more than once to get a really clear liquid. After re-bottling, a few fresh ingredients can be added, both for decoration and identification. The bottles should then be re-sealed.

How to seal and store
Seal the bottles tightly with non-corrosive, screw-top lids, or new corks. Corks are only suitable for short-term storage, and they must be sterilized. After trimming the corks to fit the bottles, sterilize them in boiling water for a few minutes; this also softens them slightly. To seal, pound the corks into the necks of the bottles with a wooden mallet, leaving only 5 mm (¼ inch) exposed cork. Flavoured vinegars should keep for about 12 months if the vinegar has been strained. If a large quantity of fresh herbs or garlic has been used, and the vinegar has not been strained, the shelf life will be shorter.

What can go wrong and why
The vinegar can ferment if it is kept too warm. A low storage temperature is also important for maintaining the flavour. Discard fermented vinegars or any that develop a questionable colour or flavour. Vinegar can evaporate from the bottle if it has not been sealed tightly enough.

BLUEBERRY-HERB VINEGAR

Colour and flavour pervade this distinguished vinegar, which combines plump blueberries, basil, and pink-tinted chive flowers. You can use one variety of basil, or a selection of sweet green and deep purple opal basil. For an elegant finishing touch, decant the vinegar into tall decorative bottles.

INGREDIENTS

1 large bunch of fresh basil

450 g (1 lb) blueberries

1 litre (1³/₄ pints) white wine vinegar

15 ml (1 tbsp) chopped fresh chives

fresh chive flowers and blueberries, to finish

Makes about 900 ml (1 ¹/₂ pints)

1 ▲ Strip the basil leaves from their stalks. Tear the leaves into small pieces. Discard the stalks.

2 ▲ Put the blueberries and a little vinegar into a non-metallic bowl. Crush the berries with the back of a wooden spoon to release their juices.

Stir lightly to mix colours and flavours

3 ◄ Stir in the remaining vinegar, the basil, and the chopped chives. Pour the mixture into a large sterilized jar. Seal and shake well. Keep in a cool dark place for 4 weeks before using, to allow the flavours to develop. Shake the jar from time to time.

4 ► Line a funnel with a double layer of muslin. Strain the flavoured vinegar through it into sterilized bottles, to within 3 mm (¹/₈ inch) of the tops. Add a fresh chive flower and a few blueberries to each bottle to give an attractive finish. Seal and label. The vinegar is now ready to use.

Herbs of Provence Vinegar

INGREDIENTS

4 large sprigs of fresh rosemary

4 large sprigs of fresh tarragon

4 sprigs of fresh thyme

6 fresh bay leaves

2 pinches of fennel seeds

1 litre (1 3/4 pints) red wine vinegar

Aromatic flavours from the south of France are combined here to give red wine vinegar a regional taste.

1 Lightly bruise the rosemary, tarragon, thyme, and bay leaves to release their flavours. Put all the herbs and the fennel seeds into a sterilized jar, then pour in the vinegar.

2 Seal the jar and shake well. Keep in a cool dark place for 2–3 weeks before using, to allow the flavours to develop. Shake the jar from time to time.

3 Line a funnel with a double layer of muslin. Strain the flavoured vinegar through it into sterilized bottles, to within 3 mm (1/8 inch) of the tops. Seal the bottles and label. The vinegar is now ready to use.

Makes about 1 litre (1 3/4 pints)

DID YOU KNOW?
The word vinegar comes from the French *vinaigre*, or sour wine. Half of the wine vinegar produced in France comes from the city of Orléans in the Loire valley.

Spiced Blackberry Vinegar

INGREDIENTS

1 kg (2 lb) blackberries

2 cinnamon sticks

10 ml (2 tsp) allspice berries

10 ml (2 tsp) whole cloves

600 ml (1 pint) white wine vinegar

450 g (1 lb) sugar

a few fresh blackberries, to finish

1 Pick over the blackberries, removing any mouldy or damaged parts. Break the cinnamon sticks into pieces. Put all the spices on a square of muslin and tie up tightly with a piece of string.

2 Put the vinegar and sugar into a large saucepan. Stir over a low heat, until the sugar has completely dissolved. Add the spice bag. Bring to a boil, lower the heat, and simmer for 5 minutes.

3 Add the blackberries and simmer for a further 10 minutes. Remove from the heat and leave the blackberry mixture to cool completely. Discard the spice bag.

4 Line a funnel with a double layer of muslin. Strain the flavoured vinegar through it into sterilized bottles, to within 3 mm (1/8 inch) of the tops. Add fresh blackberries to each bottle. Seal the bottles and label. The vinegar is now ready to use.

Makes about 1 litre (1 3/4 pints)

Orange-Scented Vinegar

INGREDIENTS

4 small oranges

1 litre (1 3/4 pints) white wine vinegar

freshly pared orange zest, to finish

1 Thinly pare the zest from the oranges with a vegetable peeler, without taking off any pith. Cut the oranges in half and squeeze out the juice. Put the orange zest and juice into a sterilized jar, then pour in the vinegar.

2 Seal the jar and shake well. Keep in a cool dark place for at least 4 weeks before using, to allow the flavours to develop. Shake the jar from time to time.

3 Line a funnel with a double layer of muslin. Strain the flavoured vinegar through it into sterilized bottles, to within 3 mm (1/8 inch) of the tops.

4 Add 1–2 strips of freshly pared orange zest to each bottle. Seal the bottles and label. The vinegar is now ready to use.

Makes about 1 litre (1 3/4 pints)

GARLIC VINEGAR

INGREDIENTS

16 garlic cloves

salt

1 litre (1³/4 pints) white or red wine vinegar

GARLIC STICK
For an unusual presentation, thread 2–3 peeled garlic cloves on to a wooden skewer and drop into the bottle of Garlic Vinegar.

The flat side of a chef's knife can be used to crush garlic cloves. The granular texture of a little salt helps when crushing the cloves.

1 Peel the garlic cloves and lightly crush them with a little salt. Put the garlic into a large sterilized jar, then pour in the vinegar.

2 Seal the jar and shake well. Keep in a cool dark place for 2–3 weeks before using, to allow the flavours to develop. Shake the jar from time to time.

3 Line a funnel with a double layer of muslin. Strain the vinegar through it into sterilized bottles, to within 3 mm (¹/8 inch) of the tops. Seal the bottles and label. The vinegar is now ready to use.

Makes about 1 litre (1³/4 pints)

ROSEMARY AND ALLSPICE VINEGAR

INGREDIENTS

3–4 sprigs of fresh rosemary

7.5 ml (1¹/2 tsp) allspice berries

480 ml (16 fl oz) red or white wine vinegar

1 Strip the rosemary leaves from their stalks. Lightly bruise the leaves to release their flavour. Put the allspice berries in a mortar and pestle and lightly crush them, being careful not to break them up completely. Alternatively, use the end of a rolling pin to crush them.

2 Put the rosemary and allspice into a sterilized jar, then pour in the vinegar. Seal the jar and shake well. Keep in a cool dark place for 4 weeks before using, to allow the flavours to develop. Shake the jar from time to time.

3 Line a funnel with a double layer of muslin. Strain the vinegar through it into a sterilized bottle, to within 3 mm (¹/8 inch) of the top. Seal the bottle and label. The vinegar is now ready to use.

Makes about 480 ml (16 fl oz)

SPICED PICKLING VINEGAR

INGREDIENTS

2 cinnamon sticks

2 blades of mace

20 ml (4 tsp) whole cloves

20 ml (4 tsp) allspice berries

15 ml (1 tbsp) black peppercorns

1.15 litres (2 pints) cider vinegar

This vinegar is used to flavour vegetable pickles, chutneys, and even fruit pickles. It is also delicious when used with extra-virgin olive oil to make a vinaigrette dressing for salads.

1 Divide the cinnamon sticks, blades of mace, whole cloves, allspice berries, and black peppercorns equally between 2 sterilized bottles. Slowly pour in the vinegar, to within 3 mm (¹/8 inch) of the tops.

2 Seal the bottles and shake well. Label the bottles and keep in a cool dark place for 2 months before using, to allow the flavours to develop. Shake the bottles from time to time. The vinegar is now ready to use.

Makes about 1.15 litres (2 pints)

COOK'S TIP You can use the vinegar in 24 hours, rather than leaving it to mature, by heating it to just below boiling point, then pouring it over the spices. It has even more flavour if left for a week.

TARRAGON VINEGAR

INGREDIENTS

1 bunch of fresh tarragon, weighing about 25 g (1 oz)

480 ml (16 fl oz) white wine vinegar

Fresh chervil can be substituted for tarragon in this recipe.

1 Lightly bruise the tarragon to release its flavour. Put the tarragon into a sterilized jar. Pour in the vinegar.

2 Seal the jar and shake well. Keep in a cool dark place for 2–3 weeks before using, to allow the flavours to develop. Shake the jar from time to time.

3 Line a funnel with a double layer of muslin. Strain the vinegar through it into a sterilized bottle, to within 3 mm (1/8 inch) of the top. Seal the bottle and label. The vinegar is now ready to use.

Makes about 480 ml (16 fl oz)

BOUQUET OF HERBS VINEGAR

INGREDIENTS

4 large sprigs each of fresh parsley, rosemary, tarragon, and thyme

12 black peppercorns

4 celery sticks

4–6 shallots, depending on size

1 litre (1 3/4 pints) white wine vinegar

1 Lightly bruise the herbs to release their flavour. Lightly crush the peppercorns in a mortar and pestle, being careful not to break them up completely. Alternatively, use the end of a rolling pin to crush them. Thinly slice the celery and shallots.

2 Put all the flavourings into a large sterilized jar, then pour in the vinegar. Seal the jar and shake well. Keep in a cool dark place for 2–3 weeks before using, to allow the flavours to develop. Shake the jar from time to time.

3 Line a funnel with a double layer of muslin. Strain the flavoured vinegar through it into sterilized bottles, to within 3 mm (1/8 inch) of the tops. Seal and label the bottles. The vinegar is now ready to use.

Makes about 1 litre (1 3/4 pints)

ROSY RASPBERRY VINEGAR

INGREDIENTS

450 g (1 lb) raspberries

480 ml (16 fl oz) white wine vinegar

50 g (2 oz) sugar

a few fresh raspberries, to finish

This is a concentrated vinegar that should be used sparingly. The addition of raspberries yields a delicious flavour and colour.

1 Pick over the raspberries and remove any mouldy or damaged parts. Put the berries and a little vinegar into a non-metallic bowl. Crush the berries with the back of a wooden spoon, to release their juices. Stir in the remaining vinegar.

2 Pour the mixture into a sterilized jar. Seal the jar and shake well. Keep in a cool dark place for 2 weeks before using, to allow the flavours to develop. Shake the jar from time to time.

3 Line a funnel with a double layer of muslin. Strain the flavoured vinegar through it into a small saucepan. Stir in the sugar and simmer over a low heat for 10 minutes. Allow to cool.

4 Pour the sweetened vinegar into a sterilized bottle, to within 3 mm (1/8 inch) of the top. Add a few fresh raspberries to the bottle. Seal the bottle and label. The vinegar is now ready to use.

Makes about 300 ml (10 fl oz)

HERBS & SPICES

HERB & SPICE BLENDS

HERBS AND SPICES add flavour and variety to foods that would be very dull without them. Herbs have many virtues: they contribute vitamins to our daily fare, they originate from all over the world but seldom fail to adapt to different soils and climates, and they often have a natural culinary affinity for each other. The classic combination of herbs found in most kitchens – a few stalks of parsley, a sprig of thyme, and a bay leaf, all tied together with a piece of thread or string – is known by French chefs as a *bouquet garni*. If the herbs are dried they are wrapped in a square of muslin and tied with string. Another popular combination in France is *herbes de Provence*, a mixture of the herbs that grow in the hills of this southern region of France, so it is especially good in dishes from the Mediterranean.

Spices, close kitchen companions of herbs, are more robustly flavoured and more exotic because many are from the tropics. Although very different in nature, they combine successfully with sugar. Spices are used in cakes and biscuits, to flavour wine punches, and particularly in Asian cooking. They are an essential component of curries, and they season cuisines worldwide. Herb and spice blends give every cook a veritable battalion of kitchen condiments for livening up their dishes.

MAKING HERB & SPICE BLENDS

❧ Select the ingredients. Buy herbs and spices at a shop where you know there is a high turnover, so that they are really fresh. If possible, grow and dry your own herbs.
❧ Prepare the herbs or spices. Crumble dried herbs between your fingers or crush them with a rolling pin. Large amounts are easier to crush if put in a plastic bag first. Process dried spices in a mortar and pestle or in an electric grinder. Alternatively, the end of a rolling pin can be used for crushing spices. This treatment also helps to prevent peppercorns, allspice berries, and coriander seeds from getting stuck in the blades of the grinder. Occasionally, the mixed herbs and spices are dry-fried before they are ground; this helps to extract the full flavour of the ingredients.
❧ Mix the herbs or spices in a bowl. Do not stir too vigorously or the powders will make you sneeze. Spoon the mixture into small sterilized jars (see page 11), packing it down well by tapping the bottom of the jar

on the work surface. A hand-made funnel placed in the top of the jar makes the job of spooning in spices easier.

How to seal and store
Seal the jars tightly with screw-top lids. These are the best choice for keeping herb and spice blends fresh. Corks can also be used, trimmed to fit the necks of the jars, and they look attractive, but the spices will lose their flavour more quickly. Keep the jars in a cool dark place, for up to 4–6 months for herb and spice blends, and up to 1 year for flavoured sugars.

What can go wrong and why
If the herb and spice blends lose their colour and flavour, they have been stored for too long or incorrectly. Unless they are kept in dry conditions in completely airtight containers, the flavoured salts and sugars will become compact and will not pour freely.

Aromatic Garam Masala

The blending of spices is an integral part of all Indian cooking. In northern India, the most important mixture of spices is known as garam masala: "masala" literally means a "blend". Each cook creates his or her own blend, making it fiercely fiery or subtly aromatic, from a selection of two or three spices to sometimes over a dozen. This mild mix, dominated by the scent of cardamom, is ideal for meat curries.

Ingredients

20 green cardamom pods

3 cinnamon sticks

4 dried bay leaves

30 ml (2 tbsp) black peppercorns

20 ml (4 tsp) cumin seeds

10 ml (2 tsp) whole cloves

10 ml (2 tsp) freshly grated nutmeg

Makes about 40 g (1 1/2 oz)

1 Split open the cardamom pods with a small sharp knife and remove the dark brown seeds. Discard the pods and crush the seeds in a mortar and pestle. Alternatively, use the end of a rolling pin to crush them.

2 ◄With your fingers, break the cinnamon sticks into fairly small lengths. Crumble each dried bay leaf into several small pieces.

Stir and shake the pan frequently when frying the spices, to keep them on the move and prevent them from burning

3 ►Put all the spices, except the nutmeg, into a heavy frying pan. Dry-fry them over a medium heat for 2–3 minutes. Remove the pan from the heat and put the spices into a small bowl. Allow to cool, and stir in the grated nutmeg.

4 ◄Put the spices, in small batches, into an electric grinder and grind to a fine powder. (Traditionally, masalas are ground in a mortar and pestle, but an electric grinder is quicker and easier.) Pack the spice mix into a sterilized jar, seal, and label.

Kashmiri Masala

INGREDIENTS

8 green cardamom pods

1 cinnamon stick

30 ml (2 tbsp) cumin seeds

15 ml (1 tbsp) black peppercorns

10 ml (2 tsp) whole cloves

10 ml (2 tsp) caraway seeds

5 ml (1 tsp) freshly grated nutmeg

The fragrance of cardamom permeates Kashmiri Masala, a blend of spices from the northernmost valleys of India. Green cardamoms have the most delicate flavour, while the brown have an unpleasant taste and should not be used. This masala is good for chicken and lamb curries.

1 Remove the seeds from the cardamom pods and crush them in a mortar and pestle. Alternatively, use the end of a rolling pin. Break the cinnamon stick into several pieces.

2 Put all the spices, except the nutmeg, into a heavy frying pan and dry-fry over a medium heat for 2–3 minutes. Allow to cool.

3 Put the whole spices, and the nutmeg, into an electric grinder and grind to a fine powder. Alternatively, use a mortar and pestle. Pack into a sterilized jar, seal, and label.

Makes about 30 g (1¼ oz)

Chaat Masala

INGREDIENTS

6 dried red chillies

90 ml (6 tbsp) cumin seeds

90 ml (6 tbsp) coriander seeds

20 ml (4 tsp) black peppercorns

"Dry-frying" whole spices in a frying pan to a dark brown colour before grinding, as in this masala recipe, extracts their full flavour and heightens their aroma.

1 Break the chillies into pieces. Dry-fry all the spices in a heavy frying pan over a medium heat until the seeds start to pop and colour. This takes 2–3 minutes. Remove the spices from the heat so that they do not burn. Allow to cool.

2 Put all the spices into an electric grinder and grind to a fine powder. Alternatively, use a mortar and pestle. Pack into a sterilized jar, seal, and label.

Makes about 65 g (2½ oz)

Pickling Spice

INGREDIENTS

4 blades of mace

2 cinnamon sticks

2 small dried red chillies

2 small pieces of dried root ginger

30 ml (2 tbsp) allspice berries

30 ml (2 tbsp) whole cloves

30 ml (2 tbsp) coriander seeds

30 ml (2 tbsp) mustard seeds

30 ml (2 tbsp) black peppercorns

In European cooking, the idea of mixing different spices together to make a blend has fallen from favour over the years, with cooks preferring to use spices individually. One of the mixes that has retained its popularity is Pickling Spice, used to liven up the flavour of chutneys, pickles, and vinegars.

1 Break the mace blades, cinnamon sticks, and chillies into pieces, and chop the ginger root. Put all the spices into a bowl and stir. Pack into a sterilized jar, seal, and label.

2 To use, put the measured spices on a square of muslin and tie up tightly with a long piece of string. Add to the recipe when specified. Remove the bag after pickling.

Makes about 40 g (1½ oz)

VARIATION Proportions and types of spices for this traditional English recipe can vary. Fennel seeds can be added, and a pinch of freshly grated nutmeg can replace the mace.

FIVE-SPICE POWDER

INGREDIENTS

2 cassia sticks

6 star anise

15 ml (1 tbsp) whole cloves

15 ml (1 tbsp) fennel seeds

15 ml (1 tbsp) anise seeds or Szechuan pepper or whole black peppercorns

When blended together according to an ancient formula, these five spices create a harmonious mix of bitter, sweet, sour, and salty flavours. The pungent taste of Five-Spice Powder permeates many Chinese and Vietnamese roast meat and poultry dishes.

1 Break the cassia sticks into several pieces.

2 Put all of the spices into an electric grinder and grind to a fine powder. Alternatively, use a mortar and pestle.

3 Pack into a sterilized jar, seal, and label.

Makes about 25 g (1 oz)

VARIATION Cinnamon can be used instead of cassia. Use slightly more because the taste is milder.

QUATRE EPICES

INGREDIENTS

45 ml (3 tbsp) white peppercorns

5 ml (1 tsp) whole cloves

20 ml (4 tsp) freshly grated nutmeg

15 ml (1 tbsp) ground ginger

Like the Pickling Spice mix, this French blend of four spices can vary in its composition. Allspice and cinnamon can be substituted for any of the spices in this recipe.

1 Put the peppercorns and cloves in an electric grinder and grind to a fine powder. Alternatively, use a mortar and pestle.

2 Put into a bowl and mix with the freshly grated nutmeg and the ground ginger.

3 Pack into a sterilized jar, seal, and label.

Makes about 40 g (1½ oz)

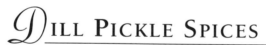

DILL PICKLE SPICES

INGREDIENTS

2 small red chillies

4 dried bay leaves

1 small piece of dried root ginger

45 ml (3 tbsp) mustard seeds

15 ml (1 tbsp) dill seeds

15 ml (1 tbsp) coriander seeds

10 ml (2 tsp) black peppercorns

5 ml (1 tsp) allspice berries

5 ml (1 tsp) whole cloves

2.5 ml (½ tsp) fennel seeds

The dainty dill seed, with a flavour reminiscent of caraway, is the special ingredient for Dill Pickle Spices. Use this blend for pickled cucumber or dill pickles, pickled gherkins, or in flavoured vinegars.

1 Break the chillies and bay leaves into pieces. Chop the ginger. Mix all the spices in a bowl.

2 Pack into a sterilized jar, seal, and label.

Makes about 50 g (2 oz)

Left to right,
Quatre Epices, Kashmiri Masala, Dill Pickle Spices

ALL-AMERICAN BARBECUE MIX

INGREDIENTS

30 ml (2 tbsp) each of dried parsley and chives

15 ml (1 tbsp) each of dried mint, thyme, and tarragon

30 ml (2 tbsp) freshly ground black pepper

5 ml (1 tsp) paprika

1 Put all of the ingredients into a bowl and mix together well, making sure to lightly crush the dried herbs into several pieces.

2 Pack the mixture into a sterilized jar. Seal the jar and label. The barbecue mix is now ready to use.

Makes about 25 g (1 oz)

VARIATIONS Different dried herbs and spices, such as rosemary, cumin, and chilli, can be used to make this mix. Other flavourings like honey and mustard can also be added to the mix, which is sprinkled directly on to meat and poultry while barbecuing.

SEVEN SEAS SPICE MIX

INGREDIENTS

15 green cardamom pods

1 cinnamon stick

30 ml (2 tbsp) coriander seeds

2 dried red chillies

15 ml (1 tbsp) cumin seeds

10 ml (2 tsp) each of celery seeds and whole cloves

This fragrant mix is an excellent flavouring for Indonesian, Malaysian, and Korean dishes.

1 Remove the seeds from the cardamom pods and crush them in a mortar and pestle. Alternatively, use the end of a rolling pin. Break the cinnamon stick into several pieces.

2 Put all the spices into an electric grinder and grind to a fine powder. Alternatively, use a mortar and pestle. Pack spice mixture into a sterilized jar. Seal the jar and label. The spice mix is now ready to use.

Makes about 40 g (1¹/₂ oz)

TARRAGON SALT

INGREDIENTS

1 bunch of fresh tarragon, weighing about 50 g (2 oz)

115 g (4¹/₂ oz) sea salt

1 Set the oven to its lowest temperature. Strip the tarragon leaves from the stalks. Discard the stalks. Coarsely chop the leaves and mix with the salt in a blender until the leaves are finely chopped.

2 Spread the leaves out on a baking sheet covered with aluminium foil. Put in the oven with the door ajar and leave for 1¹/₂ hours, or until crisp and dry. Allow to cool.

3 Pack the salt into sterilized jars. Seal the jars and label. The tarragon salt is now ready to use.

Makes about 150 g (5 oz)

SEASONING SALT

INGREDIENTS

75 g (3 oz) sea salt

7.5 ml (1¹/₂ tsp) each of ground celery seeds, white pepper, cumin, and paprika or cayenne pepper

This is an important condiment for marinating meats.

1 Put all the ingredients into a bowl and mix together well.

2 Pack into sterilized jars. Seal the jars and label. The seasoning salt is now ready to use.

Makes about 90 g (3¹/₂ oz)

ITALIAN SEASONING

INGREDIENTS

8–12 dried bay leaves

45 ml (3 tbsp) each of dried oregano, thyme, and sage

45 ml (3 tbsp) each of freshly ground pepper and paprika

1 Crush the bay leaves with a rolling pin until they are broken into quite fine pieces. Alternatively, use a mortar and pestle. Put them with all the remaining ingredients into a bowl and mix together well.

2 Pack into a sterilized jar. Seal the jar and label. The Italian seasoning is now ready to use.

Makes about 40 g (1¹/₂ oz)

HERBES DE PROVENCE

INGREDIENTS

60 ml (4 tbsp) each of dried oregano, savory, thyme, marjoram, and rosemary

In Provence, dried herbes de Provence are sold in little terracotta pots topped with the local patterned cloth, or in brightly coloured bags of the same material. By a simple blending of five herbs, you can make your own blend, for adding authenticity to any Provençal dish.

1 Put all the herbs into a bowl and mix together well.

2 Pack into a sterilized jar. Seal the jar and label. The herbs are now ready to use.

Makes about 20 g (³/₄ oz)

BOUQUET GARNI

INGREDIENTS

12 dried bay leaves

60 ml (4 tbsp) dried thyme

60 ml (4 tbsp) dried parsley

30 ml (2 tbsp) dried celery leaves

This French blend is usually tied together in a muslin square when dried ingredients are used. The bundle should always contain a bay leaf, thyme, and parsley. Sometimes other herbs, like chervil, savory, or tarragon, are added. Celery leaves can also be used.

1 Crush the bay leaves with a rolling pin until they are broken into quite fine pieces. Alternatively, use a mortar and pestle. Put them with the remaining herbs into a bowl and mix together.

2 Cut a double thickness of muslin into 7.5 cm (3 inch) squares. Put 15 ml (1 tbsp) mixture on each square of muslin and tie up into bags with string. Pack the bags into sterilized jars. Seal the jars and label. The bouquets garnis are now ready to use.

Makes about 15 g (¹/₂ oz), enough for 12 muslin bags

ENGLISH MIXED HERBS

INGREDIENTS

90 ml (6 tbsp) each of dried parsley, chives, thyme, and tarragon

This is the English version of herbes de Provence. It is a wonderful complement for lamb, pork, or stuffing. Rosemary, sage, and marjoram can be used in addition, or as substitutes.

1 Put all the herbs into a bowl and mix together well.

2 Pack into a sterilized jar. Seal the jar and label. The mixed herbs are now ready to use.

Makes about 25 g (1 oz)

MIXED SPICES

INGREDIENTS

2 cinnamon sticks

30 ml (2 tbsp) coriander seeds

10 ml (2 tsp) each of allspice berries and whole cloves

22.5 ml (1¹/₂ tbsp) ground ginger

5 ml (1 tsp) freshly grated nutmeg

This blend is also known as pudding spice, and has been popular in English cooking since the sixteenth century. Few traditional mixtures have survived as long. Use it in puddings, cakes, and biscuits.

1 Break the cinnamon sticks into several pieces. Put with the coriander, allspice, and cloves into an electric grinder and grind to a fine powder. Alternatively, use a mortar and pestle.

2 Put the spice mixture into a bowl and stir in the ginger and nutmeg. Pack into a sterilized jar. Seal the jar and label. The spices are now ready to use.

Makes about 25 g (1 oz)

VANILLA SUGAR

INGREDIENTS

1 kg (2 lb) caster sugar

4 vanilla pods

As this vanilla sugar is used up, in custards, cakes, and milk puddings, keep the jar topped up with fresh caster sugar. It will continue to absorb the vanilla flavour from the pods.

1 Divide the sugar between 2 sterilized jars. Press 2 vanilla pods down into the sugar in each jar.

2 Seal the jars and label. Keep in a cool dark place for 1 week before using, to allow the flavours to develop.

Fills two 450 g (1 lb) jars

CINNAMON SUGAR

INGREDIENTS

1 kg (2 lb) caster sugar

100 g (4 oz) cinnamon sticks

1 Divide the sugar between 2 sterilized jars. Divide the whole cinnamon sticks evenly between the jars and press the sticks down into the sugar.

2 Seal the jars and label. Keep in a cool dark place for 1 week before using, to allow the flavours to develop.

Fills two 450 g (1 lb) jars

ORANGE OR LEMON SUGAR

INGREDIENTS

6 oranges or 8 lemons

1 kg (2 lb) caster sugar

1 Set the oven to its lowest temperature. Peel the zest from the fruit with a vegetable peeler. You will need about 100 g (4 oz) zest. Spread the zest out on a baking sheet covered with aluminium foil. Put in the oven and leave for about 3 hours, or until dried out. Let the zest cool.

2 Divide the sugar between 2 sterilized jars, layering it with the dried zest. Seal the jars and label. Keep in a cool dark place for 1 week before using, to allow the flavours to develop.

Fills two 450 g (1 lb) jars

Spice Mix for Mulled Ale

INGREDIENTS

6 cinnamon sticks

12 pieces of dried lemon zest (see box, page 110)

6 whole nutmegs, cut in half

36 whole cloves

To make mulled ale: use 1 bag of spice mix for each 600 ml (1 pint) ale.

1 Cut a double thickness of muslin into 12 pieces, each 5 cm (2 inch) by 7.5 cm (3 inch).

2 Break each cinnamon stick into 2 pieces. Put 1 piece each of cinnamon and lemon zest with half a nutmeg and 3 cloves on each piece of muslin. Gather the muslin into small bundles and tie up tightly into bags with string. Pack the bags into sterilized jars. Seal the jars and label. The spice bags are now ready to use.

Makes about 50 g (2 oz), enough for 12 muslin bags

Spice Mix for Glühwein

INGREDIENTS

24 small pieces of dried root ginger

90 ml (6 tbsp) allspice berries

24 whole cloves

WINTER WARMER
Glühwein *is the perfect beverage when the weather is cold.*

This German spice blend is traditionally used to make Glühwein.

1 Put all of the spices into a bowl and mix together well.

2 Pack into sterilized jars. Seal the jars and label. The spice mix is now ready to use.

Makes about 50 g (2 oz)

To Make *Glühwein* Pour 2 bottles of red wine into a saucepan, and add 45 ml (3 tbsp) sugar. Simmer over a low heat, stirring with a wooden spoon, until the sugar has completely dissolved. Do not allow the mixture to boil. Add 45 ml (3 tbsp) *Glühwein* spices, 1 sliced orange and 1 sliced lemon. Heat to just below boiling point. Taste and add more sugar, if necessary. Leave the *Glühwein* to stand for 1 hour, then reheat and serve. Makes 6–8 servings.

Orange Spice Mix

INGREDIENTS

12 cinnamon sticks

24 whole cloves

45 ml (3 tbsp) allspice berries

12 pieces of dried orange zest (see box, page 110)

1 Break each cinnamon stick into 2 pieces. Put the broken cinnamon sticks with the remaining ingredients into a small bowl and mix together well.

2 Pack the mixture into sterilized jars. Seal the jars and label. The spice mix is now ready to use.

Makes about 75 g (3 oz)

COOK'S TIP When infusing these spices in punches, allow 30 ml (2 tbsp) mixture for each 600 ml (1 pint) liquid. Tie up the spices into a muslin bag, so the spices do not have to be strained out.

FINISHING
TOUCHES

DECORATING BOTTLES

Glass bottles can be transformed into rustic, romantic, vibrant, or psychedelic creations by a little paintwork, stencilling, or spraying. All you need are metallic spray paints, waterproof felt-tip pens, sable-hair brushes, and specially formulated glass paints, which are all available in good craft shops. Use clean dry bottles so that the paint will adhere properly. Hand-made paper collars are an original finishing touch.

Above left, hand-painted bottle; above right, negative-stencilled bottle

POSITIVE STENCILLING

Fix a stencil on to the bottle and spray with metallic spray paint, to simulate an etched or antique glass effect. Be sure to cover all other surfaces of the bottle with adhesive tape, protecting surfaces with newspaper, and your hands with rubber gloves. When the paint is dry, remove the tape and stencil. Any blurred edges can be cleaned up with a razor blade or with a little nail polish remover.

NEGATIVE STENCILLING

Stick self-adhesive motifs, or shapes made from masking tape, all around the bottle to create a pattern. Stick the edges down well, or paint will seep underneath. Protect the top of the bottle with tape. Spray the entire bottle with metallic spray paint, leave for 30 minutes, and spray with a second coat. When the paint is dry, carefully remove the motifs to reveal the pattern on the bottle.

A WORD OF CAUTION

Always work with metallic spray paints in a well-ventilated area, preferably outside. Protect all surrounding surfaces and wear rubber gloves.

PAINTING BOTTLES

Use formulated glass paints or waterproof felt-tip pens to decorate bottles. Try simple patterns before graduating to more complicated designs. Apply the paints in one stroke because they dry quickly. Some thinners that delay drying times are available, but use sparingly. Highlight the design on the bottle by attaching white card to the other side, removing the card for the finishing touches. Delicate hand-painted surfaces can be protected with a coat of clear craft varnish.

FINISHING TOUCHES
Silk ribbons and braids look beautiful tied around bottles; they are also useful for attaching tags and covers to bottles.

MAKING COVERS AND COLLARS

Covers for bottles can be made with material or metallic crêpe paper. Cut a circle from the material or paper and tie on to the top of the bottle with a large ribbon or cord. Collars, made from card, are more difficult: draw a template in the shape shown below, on to the reverse of some coloured card. Cut out the template. Lightly score along the dotted lines and bend the card. Glue or tape the angled end to the inside of the opposite end, to fasten and slip over the bottle neck.

PRETTY AS A PICTURE
Spray-painted and hand-painted bottles look artistic when finished with a collar or decorated with leaves and braiding.

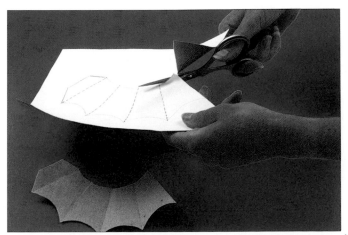

135

DECORATING JARS

Gift wrapping does not need to cost a fortune if you hunt in the right places. Liven up a humble jar with a spray of découpage cherries, a leaf-wrapped lid, or a bright strip of Petersham ribbon sealed with wax. Alternatively, a cotton bandeau ribbon or a silk cord can be tied around the jar to make it look extra special.

PICTURESQUE PRESERVES
Paper cut-outs can turn preserves into fancy gifts. They look beautiful and also indicate what is inside.

DÉCOUPAGE

Decorating surfaces with paper cut-outs is known as découpage. Cut out fruit or vegetable pictures from magazines, keeping the edges neat (a sharp scalpel is best for this task). Coat the back of the cut-out with paper adhesive, and position decoratively on the jar or lid.

COVERING LIDS WITH LEAVES

Wash and dry large leaves, such as Virginia creeper, sycamore, or maple. Paint the dry leaves on both sides with glycerine (available from chemist's shops). Arrange them on the top of the lid, wrap with cling film, and secure with a rubber band. Weight the lid and leave in the refrigerator overnight. Gently unwrap, and wipe off any excess glycerine. Secure the leaf on the lid with a piece of raffia.

MAKING A WAX SEAL

Wrap ribbon around the jar and hold temporarily in place with masking tape. Use a taper to light a stick of sealing wax and hold it about 2.5 cm (1 inch) away from the point to be sealed. Let the wax drip steadily until a 2.5 cm (1 inch) wide blob has formed. If the flame goes out, re-light the wax and continue. Before the wax has time to cool, press a decorative metal seal down firmly on the melted wax, and hold it there for a few seconds until a good impression has been left. Remove the masking tape. *Note: it is a good idea to practise making your seals beforehand with spare ribbon on empty jars.*

SEALING WITH WAX
A variety of decorative metal seals and wax sticks are available from specialist stationery shops.

__Far right__, wax seals add a professional touch to gifts; __right__, leaf-wrapped lids are an unusual but natural covering for jars

PRESENTATION IDEAS

A beautifully presented preserve is a pleasure both to give and receive. Here are some imaginative and innovative ways to make your gifts look elegant and stylish.

ALL WRAPPED UP
Make your own gift bags with wallpaper and string, and place preserves inside in a straw "nest". Or, cover with unbleached linen and tie with raffia.

IN THE BAG
Use clear paper adhesive to stick shells and starfish on to bottle bags. Rest bottles in shredded tissue.

HAT TRICK
Wrap hat netting around a bottle and secure with florist's wire. Decorate with braid and ribbon.

A TOUCH OF SPICE
Spice bags are made of muslin tied with ribbons or strings for gift-giving. Place several bags in a glass and wrap with patterned cellophane. Bundle up with a beautiful bow.

BOX CLEVER
Cover boxes with designer paper, pleating the edges. Use doilies and tissue to create a lavish effect.

PERFECT FIT
Cover a storage tin and lid with wood-patterned paper, snipping and folding pleats over the edges so they are neat. Adorn with silken braid and gingham tissue paper.

BANDANA WRAP
Bandanas are useful and ornamental. Knot around preserves in a basket.

CRACKING SUCCESS
Cellophane crackers are a good way to display jars of preserves, herbs, and spices.

TEA-TIME TREAT
Sit a pot of jam on shredded tissue inside a cup and saucer, then wrap in cellophane and tie with ribbon.

BASKET WORK
Wooden and straw baskets look attractively rustic. Lay preserves on a bed of straw and secure in place with wire.

LABELS & TAGS

Decorate your gifts with a label or a tag, to provide a personal touch to your culinary creations. Commercial labels, tags, and covers are available, but it is easy to design and make your own. A calligraphy pen gives a professional look.

DESIGN A TAG
Draw or paint a tag to reflect the ingredients in your preserves, to give instant recognition of their flavourings.

HAND-PAINTED LABELS
Use nature as an inspiration to create hand-painted labels. Fix to bottles or jars with paper glue or double-sided tape.

TEMPLATE TAGS
Use a template, such as a leaf or traced illustration, to make pretty shapes. Use coloured or embossed paper and cut edges with pinking shears for added interest.

EMBOSSED TAGS
Use specialized embossing tools, such as a template and stylus, to press out the initials of the gift's recipient in coloured paper.

READY-MADE GOODS
Labels, tags, and jar covers are available in shops and stores, so search around for the latest designs.

HAND-TINTED TAGS
Take photocopies of fruit or vegetable illustrations and hand tint with pens, crayons, or pencils.

140

ACKNOWLEDGMENTS

Photographers David Murray
Jules Selmes
Photographer's Assistant Steven Head
Home Economist Sarah Lowman
Reader Annelise Evans
Typesetting Debbie Lelliott
Linda Parker
Debbie Rhodes

Production Consultant Lorraine Baird
Text film by Disc to Print (UK) Limited

Carroll & Brown Ltd would like to thank Stephen Poole, Mary
Denning, Pat Baines, and Audrey Fox for supplying produce from
their gardens for photography and Carolyn Chapman for her help
with the Finishing Touches chapter. A selection of decorative ribbons
was supplied by Panda Ribbons, c/o Wendy Crease, Topstitch
Publicity, Elm Tree Workshops, Hitcham, Suffolk, 1P7 7LJ. Labels
on pages 132 and 137 are copyright of Kate Weese, California.

NOTES

•Follow one set of measures only – do not mix
metric and imperial as they are not exact equivalents.
Metric conversions for this book have been taken from the
fourteenth edition of Home Preservation of Fruit and
Vegetables, edited by Bridget Jones, with technical
guidance from the Institute of Food Research,
published by HMSO.

•Preserving is not without dangers. Cleanliness,
equipment, timing, acidity, and a wide variety of other
factors are critical to getting results that are safe to eat.
The foods shown in this book were decanted and
photographed immediately after preparation; they are not
all in airtight containers. This book gives recipes and
guidelines only. If you wish to store foods for longer
periods, you must follow specific instructions for methods
of preserving. Dorling Kindersley assumes no responsibility
for the preserving of foods described in this book.

•Over a period of prolonged storage, the colours of some of
the preserves may fade.